1972

ZOLTÁN KODÁLY

LÁSZLÓ EŐSZE

ZOLTÁN KODÁLY

HIS LIFE AND WORK

CRESCENDO PUBLISHING COMPANY

BOSTON

LIST OF ILLUSTRATIONS

PREFACE

The inexorable process of birth and death, of renewal and decay, that underlies the whole of life, whether of Man or Nature, is reflected in the worlds of science and the arts by the recurrent controversies that mark the struggle between the old and the new, between progressive and reactionary ideas. This struggle is continuous. But it is at the turning-point between two ages, when the exponents of the new ideas are not merely impatient rebels but men of genuine talent, that the struggle reaches its height. And in the field of European music the beginning of the twentieth century was such a turning-point.

In the field of European music the officially accepted giants, Richard Strauss and Giacomo Puccini, were regarded as living proof of the continued vitality of Romanticism. Yet in point of fact the romantic movement had already outlived itself and it was the counter-movement, led by their contemporaries, Janáček, Debussy and Vaughan Williams, that was to prove victorious. Of the outstanding members of this movement, four—Stravinsky, Szymanowski, Malipiero and Kodály—were born in the year 1882. They had been preceded by Schoenberg, Respighi, Pizzetti and Bartók; and Casella, Webern, Berg, Shaporin, Prokofiev, Honegger, Milhaud and Hindemith were to follow. These men constituted the main body of the army of composers that was taking up its positions at the beginning of the new century, and though most of them bore different watchwords on their banners there was one aim that united them: the rejection of the musical ideals of their immediate predecessors. How far each of them succeeded in practice in breaking the navel-string that bound them to the musical era they sprang from is another matter. The fact remains that, in their quest for inspiration, all of them turned to the distant past, in the same way that they all looked for the realization of their aims to the distant future.

But Romanticism was not yet defeated. It still refused to admit that its rich armoury of form and content was exhausted; and nowhere, apart from Germany, was the rear-guard action more stubbornly fought, perhaps, than in Hungary. At that time the centre of the Carpathian basin was a real stronghold of German music. Local experiment was completely overshadowed by the giant figures of Brahms and Wagner; the professors of the Budapest Academy of Music were German; and German was virtually the official musical language. This accounts for the fact that, at the beginning of the twentieth cen-

7

tury, the music of Debussy was completely unknown there; and that neither the Czech and Polish national schools, despite Liszt's high appreciation of them, nor the brilliant achievements of the Russian 'Five,' had found the least response. Thus the hold of German music on the narrow stratum of educated people was almost complete: the aristocracy, for the most part loyally pro-Habsburg, as well as the urban middle class, looked to the capital, Vienna, as the arbiter of musical taste; while of course, as an audience for the higher forms of art music, the semi-educated or illiterate masses were of practically no account. Such was the background to the efforts of the bold pioneers who were setting out to conquer men's hearts with "new songs for the new times."[1]

At this juncture, however, there occurred a phenomenon which, though unusual, is by no means unprecedented in the history of the arts: a simulta-neous—one might even say a concerted—offensive in every field of creative endeavour against the barriers of indifference and obtuseness, against the guardians of the spirit of the past. The first two decades of the century saw the emergence of modern Hungarian painting, as Simon Hollósy, Károly Ferenczy, Béla Iványi-Grünwald and the other members of the Nagybánya Group[2] freed themselves from the influence of the Munich School. In Hungarian literature during the same period the work of Endre Ady, Zsigmond Móricz[3] and the principal poets of the periodicals Holnap and Nyugat represented a profound revival. And lastly, with the appearance of Kodály and Bartók, the springtime of modern Hungarian music arrived.

Of all these pioneers it was, perhaps, the two last who faced the most arduous task. For while the poets had to discover new forms in order to ex-press themselves the language of literature was already Hungarian, whereas the composers had not only to create new forms but also a national musical idiom. For the Hungarian idiom of Liszt and Erkel[4] was already inadequate. Their knowledge of folk music had been restricted to those elements of it that had been popularized in the cities, while its real treasures remained hidden in the depths of remote villages. And it was this treasure that had first to be discovered before it could become the foundation for a contemporary art music. Until the whole people had been familiarized with the airs still sung by the peasants, there could be no question of a unified musical mother-tongue. To attempt this task with any hope of success men were needed who were equipped for it in every respect; men in whom professional knowledge was combined with an almost prophetic sense of vocation, and whose love and understanding of the Hungarian peasantry was coupled with a European intellectual horizon.

Zoltán Kodály and Béla Bartók were precisely such creative spirits. Their devoted work over a number of decades represents, so to speak, not only a re-conquest of their own homeland but also of the whole world—of their homeland, because it is thanks to them that the ancient, genuinely Hungarian, folk song has come into its own in the country of its origin; of the world, because to-day their compositions, inspired by and rooted in this folk music, appeal to a universal audience. To them the credit is due for the fact that the fame and significance of modern Hungarian music are to-day acknowledged far beyond the borders of their own small country, and have indeed become a part of the musical heritage of the whole world.

KODÁLY'S LIFE

As a composer and one of the founders of Modern Hungarian music, Kodály's place in the annals of music is already established by such outstanding works as the *Psalmus Hungaricus, Háry János,* the *Spinning-Room, Dances of Marosszék* and *Dances of Galánta,* the *Te Deum of Budavár, The Peacock,* and his *Concerto* and *Missa Brevis.* As a musicologist, his collection and classification of Hungarian folk songs, his comprehensive work, *The Folk Music of Hungary,* and innumerable papers on various aspects of folklore have earned for him the gratitude of scientists throughout the world as one of the leading twentieth-century authorities. As a teacher, his training of several generations of Hungarian composers, and his work in reorganizing the teaching of music in schools and in developing a flourishing school of choral singing, have established his right to the appreciation and gratitude of his country as one of the most far-sighted engineers of Hungarian cultural policy.

What is it, then, that has enabled him to accomplish single-handed a three-fold task which one might surely have expected to absorb the energies of three men? Apart from his precocious talent and the variety of his interests, the answer is to be found in his deep love for his country and its people. This it is, above all, that has given him the force to carry through an undertaking that has often demanded superhuman efforts; though undoubtedly the circumstances of his education, the influences of his home and early environment, have also played their part. The first eighteen years of his life, the years when mind and character are at their most receptive, were spent in the Hungarian countryside, and the impressions he then received have exerted their influence throughout his career.

The Years of Preparation
(1882-1905)

His father, Frigyes Kodály (1853-1926), was a railway official—a plump, reticent man of medium height, who soon won the respect of his colleagues and superiors by his honesty and efficiency. He entered the service in 1870, and by 1883 had already been promoted to the rank of station-master, in which position he continued until his retirement at the end of 1910. His life was a typical railway man's, continually on the move, particularly at the beginning of his career, in the course of his duties. He married, in 1879, Paulina Jaloveczky (1857-1935), who bore him three children: Emilia (1880-1919) in Budapest; Zoltán at Kecskemét on the 16th of December, 1882; and Pál (1886-1948) at Galánta.

It was here, at Galánta, a village in western Hungary (now Czechoslovakia) with a mixed population of 2,400 Hungarians, Slovaks and Germans, that the composer spent what he has himself described as "the best seven years of my childhood," 1885 to 1892. Here he attended the primary school, and it was to this region that he was to return later on his first expedition as a collector of folk songs, immortalizing it in his famous *Dances of Galánta* (1933). And it was with memories of his little school-fellows here that he was to compose his songs for two voices, *Bicinia Hungarica*. Indeed, his earliest musical experiences were associated with Galánta. His father was a good violinist, while his mother not only played the piano well but also had a fine voice, so that with friends occasionally contributing a flute or 'cello it was often possible for him to hear at home excellent chamber music, which thus early became a part of his consciousness. And since at school he used to listen to the songs and ballads sung by his barefooted little companions, his first musical experience included both the chamber music of the European masters and the ancient, unspoiled tunes of the Hungarian countryside. Here, too, when they were not on their travels, the children of the well-known Mihók's gypsy band would entertain him with their fiddles, so that they became known to the villagers as "Zoltán's Squeaker Band," (a phrase which, in Hungarian, also has the meaning of a "tuppeny-ha'penny gypsy band").

In 1892, the Kodálys moved to Nagyszombat (now Trnava, Czechoslovakia, but then in the north-western part of Hungary) where his father had been appointed station-master. Here Zoltán attended the archiepiscopal grammar school, and it is not surprising that his sense of history was deeply stirred by the place, for almost every building in this ancient city had historical associations; and the subject of one of his school-boy essays was the events described in the Latin inscriptions on the walls of the houses. Nagyszombat had become prominent in the period when the greater part of Hungary was occupied by the Turks.[5] In their flight from the invaders the Archbishop and Chapter of Esztergom, as well as a number of noble families, took up residence there, which led to such a spate of building that before long the town became known as "little Rome" on account of the number of its churches. A printing house was established there at the end of the sixteenth century, and in 1619 Cardinal Pázmány founded a University,[6] which was to continue for more than a century and a half. With the closing of the University in 1777, however, Nagyszombat began to decline in importance and, by the end of the nineteenth century, the population had been reduced to some 12,000, mostly Slovaks, but with Hungarian and German minorities. At that time most of the younger generation spoke Hungarian, with the result that when, in later years, Kodály found that a knowledge of the Slovak language was necessary for his work in collecting folk songs he was obliged to study it like a foreign language, out of books.

At the grammar school Kodály passed all his examinations with distinction, showing a particular proficiency in languages, and finding ample time for music after school hours. He began by studying the piano but later switched over to the violin, making such good progress that before long he was allowed to join the school orchestra. Not content with this, however, he sent away for a manual on 'cello playing, and within the space of a few years, without any master and simply through hard work and determination, he had made himself proficient in all three instruments. His creative gifts revealed themselves at an early age. The atmosphere of his home and the part he played in the orchestra and choir of the cathedral, as well as in the school orchestra, provided a valuable stimulus. He took part in the family concerts of chamber music; and, on one occasion, when some of the 'cello parts had been lost, he wrote them in, and when fresh copies of the original had been obtained it was found that his version differed from them very little. By that time he was already beginning to make a conscious effort to acquaint himself with musical literature. The first score he studied was Beethoven's *Mass in C Major*, which he followed up with Liszt's *Missa of Esztergom*; and, in the course of his researches happening one day upon Bach's *Wohltemperiertes Klavier*, he proceeded to play it right through.

Later on he was to say of those days: "At the students' services in the old church of the Invalids for a long time we sang nothing but German church music... At the Cathedral, where I used to go to High Mass on Sundays, the musical life was more intense, though, to be sure, there were a good many instruments in the orchestra for which there were no players, and the tattered old scores were left lying about all over the place. I vividly remember one day, in the stillness of the choir, picking up a broken bassoon that had been left there, and wondering how you would produce music from such an instrument and how it might once have sounded. For me that broken bassoon became a symbol of how, if musical culture was to be recreated in Hungary, one would have to build it with fragments of its past. Yet, though its orchestra may have been primitive, I have the kindest memories of Nagyszombat Cathedral. For a composer, it matters little *what* he hears: for him the important thing is that he should acquire a sense of form, since it will be he, in any case, who must fill it with content. For this reason I feel no regrets that I was educated in Nagyszombat, and not in the German-saturated musical atmosphere of Budapest or Vienna."

It was while he was still a student in the sixth form of the grammar school that Kodály made his first public appearance as a composer. He wrote an overture for the school orchestra, which was conducted by a young teacher, Béla Toldy, in February 1898. Thanks to a friend of the family, there was a notice of the occasion in the *Westungarischer Grenzbote*, a Pozsony (now Bratislava, Czechoslovakia) newspaper, in the course of which the critic wrote amongst other things: "The composition sounds well; there is a logical succession in the arrangement of the themes... The piece reveals a dynamic talent."

The turn of the century was also a turning-point in Kodály's life, for he was about to set out for Budapest and the necessity of choosing a career faced him with a difficult problem. Though his parents had been at pains to inculcate in him a love of music, they had no intention of his adopting music as a profession. They were anxious for him "to better himself," and in Hungary at that time it was pretty generally felt that the making of music was "no occupation for a gentleman." This was the view, expressed in a variety of ways, not only of friends and well-wishers of the family, but also of many whose advice had not been sought. "He ought to go in for the law," they declared. "There are always plenty of openings for a lawyer." His school teachers, on the other hand, predicted a great future for him as a scholar. The young Kodály, however, though aware of his own talent, was anxious to respect his parents' wishes, and therefore eventually made up his mind that he would study to become a teacher, and continue with his composing in his spare time.

Thus at last, full of ambitious plans and with a tremendous urge to work, the young man arrived in Budapest, to be greeted by the pulsing life of a rapidly growing city. Over the last twenty years its population had doubled, and had now reached 700,000. New districts were springing up on all sides, and new bridges were being built over the Danube, while in an attempt to cope with the increasing traffic a tramway service and an underground railway had recently been opened. Kodály soon adjusted himself to this new environment. He enrolled at the University, in the faculty of philosophy, choosing in accordance with his literary interests Hungarian and German Language and Literature as his subjects. He also took the entrance examination for the Academy of Music, causing no little stir amongst the teachers by starting his first year in the Department of Composition having already written both orchestral and chamber music. The excellent German Professor of Composition, János Koessler, who numbered amongst his pupils such masters as Dohnányi, Bartók and Weiner, was ready to admit him at once to the second year, but

14

the young Kodály, fully aware of the importance of having a firm grounding in the subject, preferred to start from the beginning. Each year he passed his examinations at the head of his class, and had soon won a reputation for his outstanding grasp of counterpoint. His end-of-term and examination compositions reveal him as still a disciple of Haydn and the romantic composers, particularly of Schubert, yet at the same time it is clear that he was already, and increasingly consciously, beginning to draw on the Hungarian motifs which he believed should be dominant in Hungarian music. On this issue he came into conflict with his Professor, who refused to regard Hungarian motifs as anything more than "ornamental material." It is a mark of Kodály's discriminating taste, as well as of his severity as a critic of his own work, that at this time he would often compose as many as ten different movements for some of his string quartets. At the end of four years of assiduous work he was awarded his Diploma in Composition, and later was granted a travelling scholarship which enabled him to accompany a small group of students, headed by Professor Károly Gianicelli, on a visit to Bayreuth. But Kodály was not yet satisfied that he was adequately prepared for the great task he had set himself, and the following autumn he returned to the Academy for a refresher course. He was now reading for his final University examinations, while at the same time coaching other students, frequenting the Opera and concert halls, and even finding time for sport.

Having by now left his father's home, he spent the years from 1900 to 1904 at Eötvös College, a training college for forty exceptionally gifted teachers, which had been founded in 1895 and named after the distinguished Hungarian writer and statesman, Joseph Eötvös (1813-1871), and was organized on the lines of the French École Normale Supérieure. Here, under the supervision of the highly qualified staff, Kodály perfected his knowledge of English, French and German; and, amongst other specialist subjects, was introduced to Sievers's researches in the music of language. As a result of his years at the University and Eötvös College he acquired the basic academic training without which, to the great detriment of the new Hungarian music, he would scarcely have been equipped for his future mission, his research in the field of folk music. Moreover, these years at the College also had a stimulating influence on his development as a composer. While still only in his second year he was called upon to write the music for the students' annual carnival, as well as the incidental music for a number of comedies, always conducting the orchestra himself.

Then, his college days over, he took a room "across the water," in Buda, where he settled down to work for his teacher's diploma, passing the examination in 1905. Here he wrote his beautiful *Adagio*, in which as yet scarcely a trace of folk music is discernible. And finally, it was here, too, that he took the momentous decision that was to lead him back to the countryside on his first expedition in search of folk songs.

The Years of Hardship
(1905-1922)

It is hardly surprising that the young Kodály, having spent the first eighteen years of his life in the bracing air of the Hungarian countryside, should have found himself suffocating in the close German atmosphere of the capital.[7] Disgusted with the futile efforts of the untalented imitators of Wagner and Brahms, the young man felt a longing for clearer forms and purer harmonies. Intuitively he knew that the Romanticism then enjoying a belated heyday in Budapest was already in decline. All over the world new movements were springing up, and everywhere research into folk music was taking on a new vitality. And as a result the momentous decision that had been slowly maturing in his mind at last took shape: as a composer he would forego the international style, and with it any prospect of rapid success, in order to blaze a new trail towards new horizons.

In this bold undertaking he was not alone. Right from the outset he knew he could count on the collaboration of a man whose brilliant intellectual gifts were to be devoted to the same aims that Kodály had set himself, his friend, Béla Bartók, whose friendship was to remain steadfast throughout his life, in good times and in bad. "From 1900 onwards," Kodály was to recall years later, "Bartók and I were both studying at the Academy of Music, although, since we attended on different days, we never met. Moreover, Bartók's retiring disposition prevented him from making friends easily, even with his own class-mates... As for myself, I was not particularly sociable either, besides being too busy to spare much time for social intercourse." It was not until they had left the Academy that they became friends, getting to know each other on intimate terms through Mrs. Emma Gruber (née Sándor), a woman of great learning and outstanding ability, whose house was a meeting-place for Hungarian musicians. The musical atmosphere here, where Professors from the Academy rubbed shoulders with young aspirants, provided a powerful stimulus to the ambitious plans of Bartók and Kodály.

The co-operation of the two men was by no means restricted to co-ordinating their methods of collecting folk songs. Bartók used to show the compositions he was working on to his friend, and came to regard Kodály, though nearly two years his junior, as the master to whom he could turn for advice.

16

Kodály's Father

Kodály's Mother

Later he was to say of this time: "For the final, and improved, versions of many of my works, I am indebted to his marvellously sure and quick judgement." And, speaking of Kodály on another occasion, he declared that "by his clear insight and sound critical sense he has been able to give, in every department of music, both invaluable advice and helpful warnings."

It was this clear-sightedness of Kodály's that was to enable them to chart a safe course for themselves through the labyrinth of "isms," back to the villages where they could learn the folk songs from the peasants at first hand; while his sound critical sense saved them from the pitfall of a narrow nationalism. Almost simultaneously they were drinking in the songs of the Hungarian peasants and the outstanding works of European written music, for as a rule their expeditions in search of folk songs were followed by visits to the principal musical centres of Europe.

Such firmness of purpose inevitably bore fruit. After his first tour, in August 1905, in the course of which he recorded some one hundred and fifty folk tunes in Galánta and its vicinity, he proceeded to write his doctoral thesis, under the title, "The Stanzaic Structure of Hungarian Folk Song." This work attracted attention from literary scholars as well as philologists, and in April 1906 he received his Ph. D. degree; while in October of the same year, at the postponed examination concert for students who had graduated twelve months previously, his symphonic work *Summer Evening* was performed. This was his formal farewell to his university and college studies. The real hard work lay ahead, for now both the problems he strove to solve and the questions he was to investigate were of his own choosing.

There followed another folk-song expedition, this time through the villages of what was then northern Hungary, preceding a six-month visit to Berlin and Paris for the purposes of study. In Berlin, he had the opportunity of admiring the celebrated Joachim string quartet. In Paris, he made the acquaintance of Romain Rolland, Jules Écorcheville and, most important of all, the music of Debussy. He proceeded to make a thorough study of the French master's work, particularly the score of *Pelléas et Mélisande*, which he admired for the clarity of its construction and the subtle nuances of its tone effects. It was not surprising, therefore, that the *Hungarian Folk Songs*, which he published jointly with Bartók, was followed by a piece written for the piano, called *Méditation sur un motif de Claude Debussy*.

When, in July 1907, Kodály returned home with the works of the French composer in his trunk he was, figuratively speaking, building a bridge between Paris and Budapest, between the new music of France and the even newer music of his own country, for at that time Debussy was virtually unknown in Hungary. Even Bartók, despite an earlier visit to Paris and his continual quest

2

for originality, had never heard his music; and later he wrote: "When, in 1907, at Kodály's instigation... I first became acquainted with Debussy's music and began studying it, I was surprised to find that pentatonic phrases such as are to be found in our folk music play an equally important part in his melodic system." For Kodály, too, this was a year of widening horizons. At the time that modern Hungarian music was being born, there emerged from the shadows of Vienna, Berlin and Bayreuth the bright figure of Paris, to exert as she had so often done before, and particularly since the French Revolution, a fresh and liberating influence. The sun of modern French music was rising behind the mountain peaks of German Romanticism, and Debussy began to overshadow Wagner and Brahms as the herald of the future.

In September of this same year, partly as a tribute to his work both as a composer and as a scholar, but even more in recognition of the strikingly good examination results attained by his pupils, Kodály was appointed as a teacher at the Academy of Music, beginning with Musical Theory, but, in 1908, taking over also the first year students in the department of Composition. His output during these years included his *Four Songs*; the *Two Folk Songs from Zobor*, *All My Days are Clouded* and *Blooming on the Hilltop*, which is written for a choir of women's voices; the sixteen songs known as *Songs*; the ten pieces included in the *Music for Piano*, as well as his *First String Quartet* and *Sonata for 'Cello and Piano*.

As these completed works were now crying out to be performed, Kodály and Bartók decided, early in 1910, to organize a joint concert of their works. But who was to play them? The obvious choice for the piano was Bartók, but it was not so easy to find 'cellists and violinists, for the established musicians were either unable or unwilling to play their modern scores. Furtunately, however, they succeeded in finding amongst the younger generation of artists four players capable of interpreting their work. The oldest member of the quartet, the 'cellist, Jenő Kerpely, though only twenty-four years of age, had already achieved some reputation abroad: the three others, Imre Waldbauer, János Temesváry and Antal Molnár, were all under twenty. These young enthusiasts spared neither time nor effort in preparing for the concert, holding nearly a hundred rehearsals; and their enthusiasm was duly rewarded. So admirable was their playing that it led to their receiving a number of invitations to give concerts abroad, so that for several decades afterwards the members of this quartet, originally brought together for a single occasion, were to tour the world, enhancing the reputation of Hungarian chamber music and popularizing the work of Kodály and Bartók. As for the public's reaction to this first brilliant performance of the new music, while a minority of the younger generation warmly acclaimed it, the majority, largely composed

18

of officials and pundits, were content to jeer and scoff. The use of folk tunes, and the unfamiliar harmonies, shocked the professional critics into vehement condemnation. Kodály was described as "a deliberate heretic"; he was reproached "for holding both thought and melody in contempt." One critic declared that, though he was employed to teach harmony at the Academy, "he completely shunned it in his own work," while others attempted to dismiss his music as being "merely pathological."

Amongst this chorus of abuse, however, there were two critics who devoted to the concert the serious attention it deserved. One of them wrote: "(Kodály's) art is, indeed, a revolutionary act, but though he has set out to storm the ancient citadels, he is not blood-thirsty... His talent as a composer is brilliantly modern, even ultra-modern, and as a craftsman he is in the highest rank." The other proclaimed that "great formal ingenuity, interesting harmonies, exuberant tonality and melodic originality, all imbued with a feeling that is profoundly Hungarian, are the main characteristics of his work performed at this concert." While the composer and musical critic, Béla Reinitz,[8] declared: "In the future, Kodály will be numbered amongst the most illustrious Hungarians. His name will be added to the list of distinguished men who have upheld the culture of our country"—a prophecy that has since been justified. For, to-day, the dates of those two first performances—17th and 19th March, 1910—are commemorated as the double birthday of modern Hungarian music.

Almost simultaneously, Kodály made his début abroad, his music being performed before audiences in Paris and Zurich in March and May respectively. Here, as in Budapest, opinion was divided, the division becoming so acute that, in Paris, the rival factions were known as "Kodálistes" and "Anti-Kodálistes." Bartók's work met with a similar reception, but abroad, as one of his letters makes clear, the majority supported them. "Kodály," he wrote, "had an enormous success. The effect of his programme was quite sensational, for here was a man emerging from complete obscurity to become one of the foremost (composers)."

These were the circumstances in which Bartók and Kodály, the "young barbarians" as they were known to the West, set out to conquer Europe. Their work had begun to attract the attention of music lovers from all over the world to what was happening in Hungary, as evidence that a new movement towards classicism was afoot, a movement whose leading exponents were seeking to give expression to what is truly great, not merely extravagantly vast, to what was not just startlingly novel, but genuinely original.

Later in the same year their field-work in search of folk tunes underwent an unexpected development. Kodály was so deeply impressed by the similarity between the pentatonic melodies Bartók was finding in Transylvania and those he himself had come across in his own expedition to northern Hungary, that he decided to join his friend. And the result of his decision was the discovery, in the small Székely villages, of a rich source of ancient Magyar music that was still flowing profusely.[9]

This highly successful year was also crowned with personal happiness, for on 3rd August, 1910, he married Miss Emma Sándor, who was to prove a loyal helpmate in all his difficulties, assisting him both in his creative work and in the collection of folk songs. Herself a gifted musician, Emma Sándor wrote music that attracted attention abroad as well as in Hungary. In addition to winning prizes in a number of competitions, many of her themes were elaborated by Dohnányi, Bartók and Kodály. Moreover, as a talented translator, she was responsible for the German versions of several of Kodály's writings.

Kodály continued to pursue his manifold activities with increasing energy. In April 1911 he went to Rome to attend the International Congress of Musicians; and on his return both he and Bartók lent their support to a movement for setting up an Association of Hungarian Musicians, with a view to founding an orchestra capable of providing adequate interpretations of modern music. Unfortunately, owing to the resistance of official bodies and public indifference, this enterprise came to nothing, but Kodály found compensation in another folk-song expedition to Transylvania, in 1912. By now, as a result of years of hard work, he and Bartók had between them collected some three thousand folk songs, and they decided that the time had come to find a publisher for them. Accordingly, in 1913, they drew up their "Plan for the New Universal Collection of Folk Songs," in which they made detailed proposals for the systematic presentation of the material and the manner of publication. They then offered their work to the Kisfaludy Society,[10] "as the body best qualified by its whole past record to produce it." However, the Society preferred to devote its funds to issuing a series of books of dubious value, despite the fact that a mere fraction of the money thus spent would have sufficed to cover the expenses of publishing the whole body of folk songs then available. As a result of such a lack of understanding, coupled with a complete absence of any state aid and the difficult times that were to follow, this great project, like so many others conceived by the two men, never materialized. In 1914 Kodály managed to visit the Székelys of Bucovina (Csángós),[11] amongst whom he discovered, still in an almost pure form, the most primitive stratum of Magyar folk music. But his intention of making a further stay in Bucovina to record the whole of the available material was thwarted. The outbreak of World War I swept away all their plans for cultural development, and eventually led to the expulsion of the Hungarians from Bucovina.

As far as possible, however, Kodály continued to pursue his activities even during the war-years, teaching at the Academy, where, since 1912, he had been a Professor, as well as making a number of collecting expeditions in 1915-16. And he also contributed a number of articles to musical and ethnographical journals, in which he laid down the lines for further research into Hungarian folk music. But it was his own creative work that remained the pivot around which his other many-sided activities revolved. The music he wrote during these years included a number of significant works, such as the *Duo for Violin and 'Cello*, the *Sonata for 'Cello Solo*, the seven songs in *Late Melodies*, *Kádár István*, *Seven Piano Pieces*, *Five Songs*, the *Second String Quartet*, and the incidental music he composed for Zsigmond Móricz's play, *Lark Song*.

Prior to the War, his work had been performed in most European countries, but now it crossed the Atlantic, his *First String Quartet* being performed in five of the principal cities of the U. S. A. by the admirable Kneisel Quartet. Yet he still continued to meet with censure and incomprehension in his own country. In 1914, a number of official bodies had founded the National Musical Society of Hungary, in opposition to the proposals for an Association of Hungarian Musicians and with the unavowed aim of disarming Bartók and Kodály. At its first performance in 1917 his *Two Folk Songs from Zobor* were greeted with unmitigated hostility, several critics even going so far as to accuse Kodály of having faked the songs, because their harmonies sounded "strange" to them.

It was only after a long interval, on 7th May, 1918, that a second concert entirely devoted to Kodály's work was given: the *Duo for Violin and 'Cello*, the *Late Melodies*, and the *Second String Quartet*. Even so, the critics still refused to recognize in this music anything more than "the eccentric, almost perverted, manifestation of a great and muscular, though misguided, talent." All the critics found something to quibble at, but each of them took exception to a different aspect of his work. While one praised his sense of form, another censured him for "his utter lack of constructive capacity." Though one critic praised the melodious quality of his slow movements, another reproached him for his scant regard for melody. Some professed to find his music too complex, others accused him of being affectedly primitive. While, in contrast to those who admired "his masterly expression of an atmosphere and savour that were genuinely Hungarian," there were others who attributed the popular intonations of his music to Rumanian influences.

The violence of these contradictions may perhaps be taken as an indication that critics and lovers of music were coming to realize that Kodály's genius was of an order that could not be broken or suppressed by a conspiracy of silence. Certainly, their effect on Kodály himself was to bring home to him that, whether as a musicologist or a composer, nothing was to be gained by retreating to an ivory tower: the difficulties involved in popularizing the musical principles he believed in must be boldly faced. Accordingly, at the end of 1917, he became the music critic of the progressive literary journal, *Nyugat*; and in 1918-19 he worked in the same capacity for the liberal daily paper, *Pesti Napló*. His incisive, tersely written reviews succeeded in dispelling a number of long-standing ambiguities, and opened up a whole new approach to the understanding of music. Whatever subject he might be writing on, he always spoke with the voice of a teacher, determined to win recognition for contemporary Hungarian music and to raise the general level of musical appreciation.

After nearly five years, the War had now entered its final phase. Hungary, as part of the Habsburg Empire, had been embroiled in it right at the start, and by now the nation's resources had been sapped by the effort of waging war on several fronts simultaneously. Among millions of war-weary, frustrated Europeans, a revolutionary mood was rapidly developing; and, in Hungary, popular discontent exploded in the autumn Revolution of 1918. By the following spring the working class had taken over, and the Hungarian Republic of Councils was proclaimed. This social and political transformation exerted its influence also in the field of the arts. The administration of music was put in the hands of Béla Reinitz, who assumed executive authority from the time of the bourgeois Revolution in October 1918; and who, in the discharge of his duties, called upon Kodály, Bartók and Dohnányi for their expert advice, appointing them as his musical Directory. At its meeting on 14th February, 1919, the Council of Ministers reorganized the Academy as the National Academy of Music of Hungary. Its former Director, Ödön Mihalovich, was retired on a pension and was succeeded by Ernő Dohnányi, while Kodály was appointed to the newly created post of Deputy Director. At the same time, Jenő Hubay, feeling slighted at being passed over, turned down an offer to take charge of an independent class for artists of the violin, and went into exile.

Kodály accepted the post at the instance of Reinitz. But he was also motivated, partly by the desire to help Dohnányi in carrying out the latter's sound projects for reform, partly because he saw it as a long-awaited opportunity of realizing one of his cherished plans, the creation of a sound system of solfeggio[12] instruction, hitherto badly neglected. Acting on behalf of Dohnányi, who was in Scandinavia, Kodály settled down to the task of improving musical training, but time was already running out. The fate of the Hungarian Republic of Councils was sealed by foreign intervention; and at the beginning of August 1919, the dictatorship of the proletariat was overthrown. With the restoration of capitalism, Kodály's initiative at the Academy was completely crushed. A witch-hunt was started against anyone who had held office under the Hungarian Republic of Councils, and it became a time for paying off old scores. Reinitz had to flee the country. But though Dohnányi was cleared, Kodály was suspended; and an enquiry into his conduct under the Republic was set on foot. Hubay returned to Hungary, determined to "restore order" by energetic action; and those teachers who had gone on strike in protest were intimidated into a resumption of their duties.

In the course of some six months, Kodály had to endure the distressing experience of twelve separate hearings before a Committee of Enquiry presided over by Counsellor Baron Gyula Wlassics (Junior) of the Ministry of Education. His principal accusers were two of his former colleagues, Professors Rezső Kemény and Béla Szabados, while the principle of impartiality was represented by the two other members of the Committee, both lawyers. The indictment was drawn up with punctilious detail, the eight charges in respect of his political actions and the discharge of his official duties being classified under two heads:

"*Part I*
i. Was a member of the Directory of Music;
ii. Had the *Internationale* orchestrated by Professors of the Academy;
iii. Gave permission for the recruitment of soldiers for the Red Army at the Academy;
iv. Delayed the hoisting of the national flag after the fall of the Republic of Councils Government.

Part II
i. Participated in strike action by teachers at the Academy;
ii. Without reference to the Committee, but in its name, issued permits irregularly for the qualifying examinations in the course for Teachers of Singing...
iii. In contravention of the Rules, used a rubber stamp on official Academy documents, instead of signing them in his own hand.
iv. On numerous occasions during his term of office as Deputy Director behaved in a manner conducive to maladministration and disorganization of the work of the clerical staff..."

His accusers were not above attempting to bring outside pressure on the Committee by influencing public opinion. At their instigation, an article by Izor Béldi appeared in the daily paper, *Pesti Hírlap*, of 7th January, 1920, in which, under the heading "Res Musicae," he wrote *inter alia*: "The staff of the Academy of Music... must be purged of those who, by their conduct under the dictatorship of the proletariat, have proved themselves to be unreliable. The adjustment of salary scales, still bearing strong traces of Reinitz's dictatorship, must be drastically revised... Every care should be taken to preserve the younger generation of musicians from the contamination of such 'ultra-modernist' movements as Symbolism and Cubism. Indeed, what these people chose to regard as the present, history has already relegated to the past. What we want is an Academy that will train *musicians,* not foster *young Kodálys...*"

Yet, despite their scheming, Kodály's enemies failed to bring him to his knees; and their failure was due in no small measure to the courageous stand taken by his friends, Dohnányi and Bartók. Both men protested to the Chairman of the Committee against the inquiry. In a letter of 28th January, 1920, Dohnányi wrote: "Responsibility for all measures taken during the specified period, apart from those of a purely administrative character... rests with the Director of the Academy. I must protest against the procedure which calls Kodály to account for actions, the responsibility for which rests, not upon him, but solely upon myself, as Director of the Academy. I wish to put it upon record that I fully identify myself with Kodály, and assume full responsibility for all measures taken under my Directorship."

On 3rd February Bartók wrote, in respect of membership of the Directory of Music: "Having myself participated in the executive functions of that body in precisely the same way as Kodály, I feel I must protest against the procedure that calls him alone to account, either for the mere fact of former membership, or for any action to which exception is now taken."

Throughout the hearings, Kodály preserved a characteristic composure, boldly repudiating all aspersions on his patriotism and on his activities in connection with the collection of folk music. "Let him who has done more for Hungary than I... come forward to lecture me," he said. "All the work I have accomplished has been done without any financial aid from the State, but with an expenditure of my own money that might almost be called prodigal. And, incidentally, (these efforts) are of a kind that cannot be paid for in money. And from where have I obtained the energy for all this? Doubtless from that 'anti-patriotic disposition' of which people are so anxious to find me guilty. I have never meddled in everyday politics. But, figuratively speaking, every bar of music, every folk tune I have recorded, has been a political act. In my opinion, that is true patriotic policy: a policy of actual deeds, not of mere phrase-mongering. And it is for this I am being persecuted."

When giving evidence at the enquiry, Dohnányi observed: "Kodály cannot be accused of unpatriotic conduct—a man who has spent his life searching out and collecting Hungarian folk songs is obviously more patriotic in spirit than many of his accusers." But the Committee held the opposite opinion.

24

As Béla Szabados put it: collecting folk songs "may well be regarded as a highly commendable pursuit, but not accepted as satisfactory evidence of a patriotic outlook, since in this case it had served to strengthen un-Hungarian, rather than Hungarian, interests."[13]

Accepting full responsibility for all his actions, Kodály declared with regard to the Directory: "As to the men with whom I had the pleasure of serving on that body, any Hungarian musician, I should have thought, would have been flattered to share the company of men like Dohnányi and Bartók." And, defending Reinitz, then in voluntary exile, he said: "Our relations were founded on mutual respect. I learned to know him as a fanatic for truth and a man of character from whom I cannot withhold my respect." Here, and in the evidence he gave in defence of Imre Waldbauer, another of those against whom disciplinary action was taken, his human stature in times of adversity was displayed to the full.

But even the most drawn-out inquiries must come to an end at last; the malicious slanders were disproved and the unfounded charges collapsed. In his ruling dated 25th June, 1920, the Minister of Education, István Haller, declared: "It has been established that neither your conduct under the Communist Government, nor your behaviour as a Professor, was in contravention of the rules governing your terms of professional service." "But," he continued, "since in your capacity as Deputy Director—i. e., as an executive officer in charge of an institution, who might therefore be reasonably expected under all circumstances scrupulously to maintain order and discipline within that institution—you not only identified yourself with the strike action organized by a number of Professors at the Academy, but, moreover, on a number of occasions condoned malpractices committeed during your term of office... I, on the recommendation of the Committee of Enquiry, herewith terminate your appointment as Deputy Director... and order that you shall be reduced to the status of Professor, as previously held by you. Instructions for the appropriate reduction in your salary will be issued separately. Furthermore... I have given orders that you, in your capacity of Professor, shall be granted leave of absence for the whole of the first term of the University year 1920-21."

The idea of sending Kodály on leave originated with Hubay and his coterie. For them, the failure to secure his dismissal represented at least partial defeat; and, unwilling to accept it, they hoped during his absence to discover other means of preventing his return to the Academy. In a series of confidential memoranda they proceeded to invent new, and revive old, slanders against him. They alleged that he was "the initiator morally responsible for the spread of disaffection within the teaching body"; that it was he "who had

25

the governing body of that institution removed"; and they disparaged his work as a teacher, maintaining that "from the pedagogical point of view it is utterly absurd to suppose that a man, who, as a composer, represents the most extremist tendencies, can effectively function as a Professor in accordance with the rules, not only laid down by the Academy but, moreover, justified by the traditions from which the masterpieces of the past have sprung." Finally, Hubay declared: "For my part, I see no possibility of harmonious and friendly collaboration with Kodály within (the Academy) . . . and therefore consider his return to his Chair both undesirable and inadvisable"; and he recommended that the Minister "should arrange for Kodály, since he is a qualified secondary school teacher, to be removed from our institution, to some humbler post; or, if that should not prove feasible, should retire him on pension."

Although by a series of intrigues, as well as by repeated extension of his enforced leave, his enemies managed to postpone Kodály's return to the Academy, he nevertheless continued to carry on his work with unabated vigour. Meanwhile, many of his former pupils, though officially assigned to other professors, continued to visit him regularly at his home, where he was able to assist them with their studies. He also went on with the collection and classification of folk songs, publishing, in conjunction with Bartók, one hundred and fifty of those they had discovered in Transylvania; and writing his fundamental study of the subject of "The Song of Argirus." To this period, too, belongs his *Serenade for Two Violins and Viola*, in three movements, in which the note of high optimism, in sharp contrast to the bitterness of his personal experience, displays the moral strength that enabled him to overcome disappointment and disillusionment. If the scurrilous attacks to which he was submitted failed to shake his equanimity, nevertheless the witch-hunting soon opened his eyes as to the nature of the Horthy regime. He realized that, under the guise of nationalism, it was merely continuing the anti-democratic policies of the Habsburgs. And this realization served to strengthen his own genuine and deep-rooted democratic convictions.

Encouraged by his public disgrace, the critics launched a fresh attack on him. When his *Two Songs* were conducted at their first performance on 10th January, 1921, by Dohnányi, they renewed the charges of laboured harmonies and lack of imagination, dismissing the piece as tedious and artificial. One paper even indulged in personalities, describing him as "an adept in the art of keeping himself in the public eye, taking care to represent himself on every possible occasion as a congenial colleague of Bartók's . . . What we recognize as genuine inspiration in Bartók, is in Kodály merely mannerism, utterly lacking in conviction; what in the former is sweepingly and powerfully individual, is nothing more than a laboured affectation of originality in the latter. Zoltán Kodály's songs… are devoid either of sincerity or of imagination. They are pompous in their construction; and they are boring to listen to."

Bartók's reaction was prompt. The following day he made a statement in the same paper, in which he declared: "Firstly, it is quite untrue that Zoltán Kodály has ever made use of me personally with a view to advancing his own interests; and, secondly, it is equally untrue that he has at any time been a cause of bitterness to me, because, on the one hand, he is in no sense one of my imitators, and, on the other, at a time when I was being persecuted he was the one who boldly, and at all times, stood by me." And in another article, published in the February issue of *Nyugat*, he came out even more strongly in defence of Kodály. "I do not regard Kodály as the best musician in Hungary because he is a friend of mine," he wrote. "He has become my only friend because, apart from his splendid qualities as a man, he is the greatest musician in Hungary. That it is I, and not Kodály, who have most benefited from our friendship is but further proof of his splendid qualities and of his self-effacing altruism."

A young music critic, who also stood up to Kodály's denigrators, Aladár Tóth,[14] went straight to the heart of the matter when he wrote: "To accuse Kodály of being 'rootless and lacking in conviction,' as do some people, in contrast to the 'autochthonous, pristine quality' of Bartók's talent, does not merely betray a superficial critical faculty: it is also extremely malicious, for it is an attempt to use one of our two greatest musicians as a stalking-horse for an attack on the other."

Gradually, however, the campaign of abuse began to die down; and, in any case, its effects were scarcely felt beyond the national borders, for, abroad, Kodály's work was almost simultaneously achieving a wider public. He even found a publisher, Universal Publishers of Vienna, who secured an option on all his work. And the effect of this contract was greatly to strengthen his position in Hungary, thus confirming Bartók's prophecy that "it is not here, but abroad, that the Kodály case will eventually be decided."

As his status in the Academy had not yet been determined, Kodály sought an interview with the Minister of Education, József Vass, at which he acquainted him with the true facts of his case and the personal motives underlying the campaign against him. The Minister promised an investigation and, this having substantiated Kodály's account of the matter, he confirmed his reinstatement. Thus, in September 1921, after two years absence, he was able to resume his task of supervising the studies of the younger generation of composers. His outstanding successes in this field give the lie to the aspersions that had been made on his capacities as a teacher. Jenő Ádám, Lajos Bárdos,

Géza Frid, Zoltán Horusitzky, György Kerényi, Mátyás Seiber, Tibor Serly, Bence Szabolcsi, István Szelényi, Viktor Vaszy and Zoltán Vásárhelyi[15] are only a few of the pupils during this period who owed their profound and comprehensive musical training to him. And, in addition to his teaching, he continued his collection of folk songs.

Meanwhile, he persisted in his efforts to vindicate himself; and, availing himself of his right of appeal, demanded a re-hearing of his case on 15th June, 1922, insisting that the new Committee of Enquiry should consist of people "in no way associated with the dispute within the Academy." After prolonged deliberation, however, his application was rejected by the Ministry.

Although during these years Kodály carried out a measure of systematic work, they were primarily a period of preparation in which he braced himself for the tasks that lay ahead. The careful revision of his earlier compositions for publication, and the arrangements he made for two concerts of his work (on 22nd October, 1922, and 15th April, 1923), suggest that he was, so to speak, taking stock of his achievement to date. That these efforts were not merely passive, but a vital and indispensable phase of his development, was to be proved by his output in the period that began in the year 1923.

The Great Creative Period
(1923-1939)

The Hungarian capital was preparing to celebrate its fiftieth anniversary, the fiftieth anniversary of the incorporation of the three towns of Pest, Buda and Óbuda into the single city—Budapest. To mark the magnificence of the occasion, the three greatest Hungarian composers, Dohnányi, Bartók and Kodály, were each invited to compose a suitable major work. Alone of the three, Dohnányi produced the sort of thing his patrons expected: a festive overture, on the themes of the three musical symbols of official Hungary—the Hymn, the Appeal and the Credo.[16] The result was, indeed, a piece of 'occasional' music, not destined to endure.

Bartók and Kodály, however, remained true to their people, and to themselves. In the prevailing atmosphere of irredentism, Bartók's *Suite of Dances* exalted the ideal of the brotherhood of nations. Kodály, taking as his theme a free Hungarian version of the fifty-fifth Psalm, by the sixteenth century poet, Mihály Kecskeméti Vég, produced one of the great masterpieces of twentieth century music, his *Psalmus Hungaricus*, a work in which the new Hungarian music reached its peak. He had come to know the poem as a student, and at this particular moment it seemed to him that both its atmosphere and its message, which his music conveys with such admirable force, were especially relevant. The *Psalmus* is the poignant confession of faith of a poet, dedicated to the service of his people and lamenting the fate that has befallen his country. And doubtless there are many passages in the sixteenth century poem that closely expressed Kodály's most intimate thoughts. For example, "Would I might dwell in the wilderness... rather than amongst them who seek to hinder me from speaking truth"; or again, "The city is borne down with wrath, and mighty is the hatred one man feels against another: it standeth conceited in its riches, and in its treachery it is unmatched."

Certainly, at this first performance, there must have been those amongst the audience—as indeed in contemporary society as a whole—who realized that here Kodály was not merely interpreting the cares and tribulations of a bygone age, but expressing through his music his own personal sorrows and sense of outrage. And to them the experience of listening to the *Psalmus* was not just that of hearing a new musical work: in it they must also have recognized the voice of their own conscience. But even those incapable of discerning this deeper significance, his consistent opponents, were compelled, however reluctantly, to acknowledge the musical worth of the new work. For the first time, the critics were unanimous in their praise. They admitted that, here, Kodály "rises to those pure and refined heights of music, which are only to be assessed by the standards of a master like Bach." They described the *Psalmus* as "a work of fascinating depths of emotion, written by a soaring imagination that leaves one both awed and spell-bound." And one critic even went so far as to declare that "it is, perhaps, the most accomplished masterpiece ever to have been achieved by a Hungarian composer."

For Kodály, the *Psalmus* marked the opening of a new chapter in his creative work. The period of chamber music was at an end, and he was about to embark on a succession of large-scale compositions. Curiously enough, however, at the same time his work was to develop in a quite different direction, one hitherto scarcely explored in Hungary—the writing of music especially for children. In February 1925, Kodály happened to suggest to Endre Borus, who taught music in a boys' school in Budapest, that he should teach his pupils the *ad Libitum* children's choral part of his *Psalmus*. After attending one of the rehearsals, his imagination was so stimulated by the sonorous quality of the boys' voices that he told Borus, "I'm going to write something for your choir. Meanwhile, in my opinion these boys are really worth taking trouble with." And a few weeks later he produced his two little masterpieces, *The Straw Guy* and *See, the Gypsy Munching Cheese*. From that time onwards his loyalty to, and solicitude for, children has continually increased, thanks partly to his personal bent, but partly also to his high sense of vocation as a teacher. Once he realized that the youth of his country was "growing up in conditions of an utter musical corruption that is worse than illiteracy," he was determined to help with his own music to lead them back to the right road.

The enthusiasm that greeted these first choruses of his at their public performance on 2nd April, 1925, convinced Kodály that he had correctly diagnosed what was wrong: the backwardness in this particular field was the result, not of the supposed lack of interest on the part either of the young people or of the public, but rather of the lack of suitable music composed for the purpose.

During these years, Kodály's reputation was considerably enhanced by the success of a number of foreign concerts. The reception of his songs by a Berlin audience in 1924 was especially memorable. Oscar Bie, the well-known music critic of the *Berliner Börsen Courier*, wrote in his review of the concert: "With these songs... Zoltán Kodály has attained a level in the art of our times at which the problems of experimentation cease to exist. To an even greater extent than Bartók, his great admirer, Kodály has assimilated the whole tradition of the past, in order to create, in the spirit of his nation, a new art that is both genuinely and daringly original; an art that is far more genuine, far greater than the Europeanized drawing-room rhapsodies that came out of Hungary in the past... Let us have more Kodály. He and Bartók are the twin peaks of contemporary music." In the same year, his *Duo for Violin and 'Cello* enthralled the audience at the Salzburg festival of modern chamber music; and, in 1925, long critical appreciations of his work were published in the Austrian *Musikbote* and the American *Modern Music*. In his book on music appreciation, M. D. Calvocoressi ranked his chamber music above any comparable work by his contemporaries; while the International Society of Modern Music invited him to be one of the three judges in a competition for which some five hundred works had been submitted.

It might have been expected that so many successes would have secured for Kodály a period of unquestioned recognition and quiet creative work. But this was not so. In 1925, and later, he was to be subjected to a number of attacks that attempted, though with less and less success, to discredit him both as an artist and as a teacher. One of these occurred in a German-language paper published in Budapest. In a vulgarly abusive account of the examination concert given by Kodály's pupils at the Academy, a journalist, Béla Diósy, wrote: "What is revealed by this group of young musicians, who now have the opportunity of expressing themselves, is a pathetic lack of talent, of invention, and of fundamental training..." And he summed up his views as follows: "The appropriate judgement on the compositions of most of Kodály's pupils is that 'one can hear them smell.' But what above all smells to high heaven is the utter failure of the directors of the Academy of Music to call a halt to its present fatal activities. It must surely be accepted as a law of nature that the guiding pedagogic principles of a great musical institution should be founded in a noble conservatism. Once a composer has learnt to stand on his own feet, he is welcome to advocate his own fallacious beliefs and, if he chooses, to follow the course of deliberate fraud. But to submit the whole rising generation to a deliberately one-sided and anarchistic influence, is nothing less than the malicious corruption of youth." Though these words were Diósy's the ideas behind them were undoubtedly those of Hubay, who, as Director of the Academy, had been forced to conclude an unwilling armistice with Kodály. That the younger man should have proved so willing a mouthpiece is, perhaps, not surprising, for his application for a post at the Academy was then under consideration; and his appointment shortly afterwards is confirmation of his success in pleasing the Director.

Now, for the first time, Kodály was determined to reply to the charges in writing, not as an advocate of his own cause but in defence of his pupils; and as the paper that published the attack refused space for his reply, he took steps to publish it, in abridged form, elsewhere. He began by exposing the falsity of Diósy's allegations, and the real motives that lay behind them, remarking censoriously: "This piece of writing... is an offence against literary taste and good manners." Then, with stern indignation but without for a moment losing his dignity, he continued: "Deprived of the influence of foreign cultures, our own culture is bound to languish and wither... Thus it is in no spirit of chauvinism that I propose to put a few questions to those who live in our midst as foreigners, like colonials amongst savages, completely ignoring, and ignorant of, the culture of Hungary. You maintain that we should continue to produce nothing but imitations of Brahms and Schumann, rejecting, even though they be better, those musicians who have been nourished on our native music. Why? Because the music of Hungary, and everything that springs from it, is hateful to you. You are ignorant of it and unwilling to get to know it... What right, then, have you to forbid us the use of our own musical idiom? To prevent us from teaching this idiom *also* in our schools, modestly, alongside the universal language of music? We allow freedom to every taste within the limits of art. But for how long do you expect us to put up with your attempts to dictate to us the foreign tastes of your foreign soul? To your conservatism, rooted in small-town Germany or international platitude, I oppose a Hungarian conservatism, nourished by a universal culture. We want to stand on our own feet, assimilating from the cultural heritage of the entire world whatever is beneficial to us, whatever will vitalize and strengthen us. It is in this way that we shall learn to express to the full our own essence. We refuse to be a musical colony any longer. We are not content to continue aping a foreign musical culture. We have our own musical message, and the world is beginning to listen to it attentively. It is not we who have invented Hungarian music. It has existed for a thousand years. We only wish to preserve and foster this ancient treasure; and, if sometimes the opportunity should be granted us, to add to it."

And in that same year Kodály had such an opportunity. In 1925, he published the first two volumes of the series, *Hungarian Folk Music*, each containing five Székely ballads and folk songs arranged for voice and piano. And at the same time he continued to work on a great new composition, *Háry János*, a musical drama consisting of five Episodes, a Prelude and a Postscript. Its first performance at the Budapest Opera House, conducted by Nándor Rékai, was a red-letter day for Hungarian operatic music. Háry, the swaggering veteran—counterpart of Plautus's *miles gloriosus* and Raspe's Baron Munchausen—is, in Kodály's words, "the symbol of the indestructible, everlasting Magyar optimism," bringing into the theatre "the truly Hungarian gift for imaginative story-telling." The opera's success with critics and public alike was immediate. It was played twelve times in its first season, and has maintained its place in the repertoire ever since. There were, of course, dissenting voices; as, for example, the critic who wrote, "it smells of the ethnographical museum... the musical score, consisting as it does of motifs artificially transplanted from folk song, has very little chance of lasting success." Such criticism, however, had little effect on the musical world as a whole; and an orchestral Suite, made up of the principle themes from the opera, has been repeatedly performed under the most distinguished conductors with increasing success.

The fact that, in addition to this opera, Kodály was producing several new choruses for children's voices, stresses his preoccupation at this period with the necessity of developing a new style of singing. He was aware not only that this was a pre-condition for a successful break-through in the field of choral music, but also that the lack of such a style was the main obstacle to a radical development of musical education. In this respect he made a special study of the laws governing the accentuation of the Hungarian language, thus discovering, one might say, its specifically musical properties—a point to which we return in a later chapter.

Meanwhile the foreign reputation of his orchestral work was continuing to grow. On 18th June, 1926, the *Psalmus* was performed for the first time abroad, being conducted at Zurich by Volkmar Andrea, with a German version of the words by Bence Szabolcsi. And before long it had been translated into eight languages, with performances in eleven cities in five different countries.

32

Nagyszombat at the End of the 19th Century

It was with the *Psalmus*, too, that Kodály began his own career as a conductor. The occasion was its performance in Amsterdam, in April 1927, by the Concertgebouw Orchestra and the Oratorium Vereenigung Choir, with Ferenc Székelyhidy (as always since 1923) singing the solo part. Incidentally, this concert is also memorable as being the first at which a foreign choir sang in Hungarian, from a specially prepared phonetic transcription of the text. So successful was Kodály's conducting that it led to a number of further invitations abroad. He conducted the *Psalmus* on 30th November at Cambridge, and four days later in London; and again in Holland the following March, where, within a fortnight, there were five performances of the *Psalmus* and three of the *Háry János Suite*.

Amongst the earliest interpreters of Kodály's music, Mengelberg in New York and Toscanini in Milan both conducted the *Psalmus*, and later added the *Háry János Suite* and other works to their repertoire. And these pioneers were soon joined by such men as Ansermet, Casals, Dorati, Furtwaengler, Koussevitsky, Molinari, Ormandy, Reiner, de Sabata, Stock, and Wood. These foreign successes in turn reacted on opinion at home, and interest in the yearly Kodály concerts grew steadily. New folk-song adaptations, admirably interpreted by Imre Palló and Mária Basilides, and especially three recent children's choruses, *God's Blacksmith*, *The Deaf Boatman*, and *Gypsy Lament*, which were performed at a recital on 12th May, 1928, were received enthusiastically, the critics showing a new appreciation of Kodály's aims. As Aladár Tóth wrote: "His struggle to create a unified musical culture, which shall enjoy European status while remaining specifically Hungarian, is undoubtedly the most heroic and the most far-reaching aesthetic undertaking in Hungary to-day."

In the summer of 1928, with Sándor Jemnitz and Antal Molnár, Kodály founded the Hungarian section of the International Society of Modern Music; and at the end of August he conducted the *Háry János Suite* in London, and the *Psalmus* at Gloucester with success. Inspired by this experience of the Three Choirs Festival in England, he made proposals early in 1929 for a similar festival to be organized for the leading choirs of the three West Hungarian towns of Sopron, Szombathely and Győr. But as the only town to respond at all favourably was Győr, the project fell to the ground. And indeed, in general he could hope for little support for his ambitious plans, since the leading posts in the various official cultural bodies were filled by the most hide-bound people. Kodály did not lose heart, however. He realized, as he wrote in an article, "Children's Choirs," that "the Hungarian public has to be raised from its state of musical torpor," and to this end "it is only from the schools that the initiative can be expected." In this respect, from the point of view of a national musical culture, his children's choruses were, perhaps, of even greater significance than his great symphonic works. Prompted by Toscanini, he therefore revised his *Summer Evening* of 1906; as well as composing a number of masterpieces for children's voices such as *The Swallow's Wooing, Dance Song* and *New Year's Greeting* and what was perhaps up to that time his supreme achievement in this genre, the *Whitsuntide*.

As a result, on 14th April, 1929, it was possible to hold a concert entirely devoted to children's choruses, five out of the thirteen being performed for the first time. It was to prove a significant event in the development of Hungarian music. Half the programme was encored, and the whole concert had to be repeated on two subsequent occasions. Even the critic of the German-language *Pester Lloyd* conceded that "to have heard these children sing... was to glimpse a national musical culture in the making." And this was, indeed, the point. For, following the capital's example, the whole country was stirring with a new spirit; a national renascence in which Kodály and his disciples had played a considerable part. For example, at Győr, György Kerényi introduced the songs and choruses into the schools, and later organized the first singing competition in which the choirs from four schools participated. At Kecskemét, Kodály's native town, Zoltán Vásárhelyi conducted a concert of these small masterpieces, a lead soon to be followed by Szeged, Debrecen and Nyíregyháza—the beginnings of a nation-wide movement.

Another important step in the same direction was the appointment of two of Kodály's former pupils, Lajos Bárdos and Jenő Ádám, as the respective leaders of the well-known and long-established Palestrina and Buda Choirs. While of even greater assistance to Kodály personally was the launching, by Gyula Kertész and Lajos Bárdos, later to be joined by György Kerényi, of a musical periodical and publishing firm, *Magyar Kórus* (Hungarian Chorus), for the publication of the works of Kodály and other composers of the modern school.

Despite all these activities, Kodály still managed to continue with his collecting of folk songs, travelling year after year through the villages and recording fresh tunes and variants. In 1928 and 1929 he helped select the material for a series of educational recordings of music, undertaken on the initiative of the Ministry; and wrote numerous articles on folk music. In one of these, "The Artistic Significance of Hungarian Folk Song," he declared: "We have no other music that lights up the recesses of the Hungarian soul in a form at once so solid and so enduring. It is *par excellence* the classical music of our country; and the evolution of Hungarian polyphonic music in the modern European sense can follow no other course." To this period, too, belong his comprehensive article on folk music for the Musical Encyclopaedia edited by Szabolcsi and Tóth; as well as the series of historical papers published under the title "Essays on the Music of Hungary." While, in 1930, he undertook a course of lectures at the Faculty of Philosophy at Budapest University, that was to continue for several years, in which, in discussion with his students, he raised various questions relating to research into folk music, and its history.

In 1930, two of his major orchestral works were presented for the first time in Budapest: in May, Toscanini conducted the New York Philharmonic Orchestra in the revised version of *Summer Evening*, which Kodály had dedicated to him; while in December the Hungarian Philharmonic played the *Dances of Marosszék*. His friendship with Toscanini was to lead to another composition, for, at a later date, when Toscanini's daughter was being married in Budapest, he asked Kodály to give her away. He not only did so, but as a wedding present he gave the young couple four Madrigals, by Italian poets of the fourteenth and fifteenth centuries, which he had set to music for female voices.

In the same years, in addition to completing the publication of the ten volumes of *Hungarian Folk Music*, he also composed *A Birthday Greeting*, written for a mixed choir, and the large-scale *Mátra Pictures*; the last two, like most of the children's choruses, being published in three languages by three different firms—Magyar Kórus in Hungary, Universal in Vienna, and the Oxford University Press. But the great musical event of 1932 in Hungary was the first performance of the *Spinning-Room*, conducted by Sergio Failoni, at the Budapest Opera on 24th April. Both the music and the libretto of this one-act opera—or, as the composer preferred to call it, "this conversation piece of life in Transylvania"—brought to the stage the purest folk art. As the critic István Péterfi was to write later: "By consistently achieving the task he had set himself—one of the greatest difficulty in a dramatic piece—*viz.* of using no words, even in the connecting passages, that did not belong to the vocabulary of folk song, Kodály was emphasizing his political aim: to be the faithful interpreter of the people." At the time, however, the critics were, as usual, divided: some hailing it as a masterpiece, others criticizing it for, amongst other things, failing to solve the problem of recitative. Yet, despite such carping criticism, his fiftieth birthday, on 16th December of this same year, was enthusiastically celebrated by almost all shades of Hungarian musical opinion. Newspapers and periodicals throughout the country and abroad, as well as those most indebted to him, his friends and pupils, united in paying tribute to his work, while a number of organizations arranged special concerts of his music.

The summer of 1933 saw yet another great orchestral work, the *Dances of Galánta*, which he wrote for the 80th anniversary of the foundation of the Budapest Philharmonic Society. Deriving his material from some old books of Hungarian dances published in Vienna about 1800, he here revived, splendid with the new colours of his brilliant orchestration, an almost forgotten world, especially the ancient recruiting dance of the Magyars, the so-called *verbunkos* music. And meanwhile he was continuing to make his decisive contribution to that "revival of choral music," of which people were by now beginning to speak, by further additions to the long list of his choral works, particularly for the "Singing Youth." This was the name, dating from a concert in Budapest on 28th April, 1934, in which fifteen hundred children from fourteen schools took part, that was officially adopted by the movement that then came into being to carry out the spirit of Kodály's teaching. The importance he attached to this movement may be gathered from an article, written in December 1934, in the course of which he said: "All the problems now confronting us can be summed up in a single word: Education. But it must be a reciprocal education. On the one hand, the mass of the Hungarian people must be given the opportunity of appreciating art music of the highest quality; on the other, the devotees of such music must not shut themselves up in an ivory tower, but clearly realize that there is another, specifically Hungarian, tradition, which has produced work as perfect in its kind, as pure and noble in its art, as the great musical tradition of the West... Choral music is the means by which this aim can be achieved, but only on the condition that the art of choral singing is reborn. The future of music lies with the mixed choir..." And, in pursuance of this practical aim, Kodály and Bartók, in conjunction with the Academy of Sciences, now began to prepare for the press the steadily accumulating mass of folk material. In two papers belonging to this period—"The Distinctive Melodic Structure of Cheremiss Folk Music" and "Popular Tradition and Musical Culture"—he gave an account of his most recent discoveries; and at the same time, in a series of lectures in Budapest, analyzed the reciprocal influence of folk music upon art music.

In the spring of 1935, as a surprise for its audience, the Budapest Opera decided to produce a ballet, based on two of Kodály's orchestral pieces, the *Dances of Galánta* and *Dances of Marosszék*. Zsolt Harsányi[17] was commissioned to write the libretto, the choreography was by Aurél Millos, the ballet-master of the Opera, and the ballet they wrote was called *A Rebel's Tale*. After the *première*, on 13th March, one critic wrote: "Despite the fact that Kodály's music expresses abstract ideas and idealized feelings, the story provided by Harsányi is simply a character sketch in a picturesque setting. Thus plot and music are at cross purposes, and the beauty of the latter gets distorted in a world of uncongenial emotions. Nor does the pageantry of the setting provide adequate compensation, for this *Rebel's Tale* is distressingly clumsy... obviously written by someone who was unable either to understand the music

36

or to adapt himself to the requirements of the choreographer." Indeed, competent opinion was unanimous that the music had been sacrificed to the Opera's current "mania for ballet." Nevertheless, the idea of providing a theatrical presentation for these two works of Kodály's subsequently proved to be practical. With a different libretto on each occasion, they were later produced at a number of theatres in Germany, with such titles as *Rhapsodische Tanzszenen*, or *Zigeunerliebe*, or *Bergbauern*.

The following year, together with Bartók and László Lajtha, Kodály directed the work of producing a new series of recordings of folk music, which was jointly sponsored by the Folklore Division of the National Museum of Hungarian History and the Folk Music Committee of the Academy of Sciences. This collection of gramophone recordings of folk music, soon to reach the number of a hundred and fifty, was the first to be arranged scientifically; and in all it comprised some five hundred songs and numerous recordings of instrumental music. In the same year, also, a number of new compositions by Kodály were performed for the first time: the double chorus for children's voices, *The Angels and the Shepherds*; the great canon, *To the Magyars*, a dynamic chorus that was at once adopted by the whole choral movement as its revolutionary hymn; his setting, for a mixed choir, of Vörösmarty's[18] *Ode to Franz Liszt*, which was the highlight of the concerts held in commemoration of the fiftieth anniversary of Liszt's death; the mixed chorus, *Mónár Anna*; and, in 1937, *The Peacock*[19] specially written for the thirtieth anniversary of the Socialist Workers' Choir. Most of these are permanent contributions to twentieth century choral music. But undoubtedly the outstanding work in 1936 was the *Te Deum of Budavár*, a counterpart of the earlier *Psalmus*, written for a solo quartet, with a mixed choir, organ and full orchestra. Commissioned by the Budapest Municipality, as part of their celebration of the 250th anniversary of Buda's liberation from the Turks, the *Te Deum* was first performed on 2nd September, in the Coronation Church of Buda Castle. It was again performed, on 13th November, at a B.B.C. concert, and soon afterwards in Switzerland, Norway and Italy.

Yet despite this growing appreciation of his work—and, in the same period, Hungarian choirs were being acclaimed in Frankfort, England and the United States for their performances of his music—Kodály's manifold activities were still subjected to attack. One of the most violent of these appeared in an organ of clerical reaction proudly calling itself *Magyar Kultúra*. "To anyone who is not blind," it declared, "it must by now surely be obvious that the Bartók-Kodály cult is rapidly being blown up into something approaching official cultural policy... We are far from wishing to question the talent, even the genius, of these two men. But this in no way entitles them, by virtue of their official position as teachers, to smuggle their music—or, more precisely, the spirit of their music—into the student body... Kodály in particular, but also in many respects Bartók, is essentially a destructive spirit, and it is this spirit of destruction that he expresses and vindicates even in his most gifted music. To fail to recognize this in their work is to be either dishonest, or incredibly naive." This heavy-handed attack did not go unanswered, and a number of indignant repudiations were published in the press. But Kodály's own reply was simply to intensify his "destructive" activities. As a Christmas present to school-children and teachers of singing he published the first volume of *Bicinia Hungarica*, a collection of sixty songs that was to introduce into the dusty class-rooms the ancient fragrance of folk music. In addition to composing innumerable choruses for children, conducting Singing Youth concerts, and lecturing in Budapest and the provinces, he was able to found a School of Hungarian Folk Music at the Academy, as well as to initiate a movement for correcting and improving the spoken language. The most important of his works of scholarship, *Folk Music of Hungary*, was also published in 1937, first as a contribution to *An Ethnographic Survey of Hungary*, and later in a separate volume. This very comprehensive essay, as well as going into a number of editions in Hungary (the later ones supplemented by Lajos Vargyas's thesaurus of examples), has also appeared in German, Russian and English translations.

During the next two years two well-known orchestras, the Concertgebouw of Amsterdam and the Chicago Philharmonic, both commissioned Kodály to write new symphonic works for their Fiftieth Anniversary celebrations. The first of these works, the *Peacock Variations*, was conducted by Mengelberg, in Amsterdam on 23rd November, 1939, and a few days later at the Hague and Rotterdam. With the second, however, the *Concerto*, things did not go so smoothly. There had already been complications when the proposal was first mooted. When the conductor of the Chicago Philharmonic, Frederick Stock, came over to Europe to make preparations for the Jubilee, he was unable to meet Kodály in Vienna, as he had intended, and had to go on to Budapest, where the musician was in hospital after an operation. But even then, though Kodály accepted the commission and even agreed to conduct the first performance, the outbreak of the War created further difficulties; and eventually the score was taken to America by Bartók, where Frederick Stock conducted the first performance on 6th February, 1941.

Inevitably, the War put an end to his frequent journeys abroad, with the result that Kodály threw himself even more energetically into the task of guiding the musical life of his country. Nor was it only through his musical activities that he strove to realize the ideal: "For a more human humanity, for a more Hungarian Hungary." Both he and Bartók were amongst the first to protest against legislation in favour of racial discrimination; and already in 1938 he had joined a number of progressive artists and scientists who signed a declaration, addressed to the Hungarian people and Parliament, advocating equal rights for all citizens. This courageous stand was regarded with considerable suspicion by the authorities, who feared any move that might be calculated to weaken the Government's bellicose policy; and it even led to several performances of *The Peacock* being banned by the police on account of its revolutionary words and stirring music.

The Educator of His People
(1940-1960)

In a lecture he delivered on 3rd December, 1940, Kodály declared: "If we really desire a new life for our country—and who is there who does not?—then we must seek regeneration through our music as well." This idea of a musical renascence, that would atone for the missed opportunities of centuries, was the driving force behind his ever increasing educational activities. In the autumn of the same year he relinquished his post in the Department of Composition at the Academy of Music in order to work in the Academy of Sciences, preparing the collections of Hungarian folk music for the press. And, since Bartók had just asked to be retired, and had left Hungary for good, this meant that the whole burden of publication fell upon Kodály's shoulders. Moreover, he still continued as Director of the School of Folk Music at the Academy of Music, as well as lecturing at the University, to the Association of Singing Teachers, and on the radio—not to mention serving as one of the jury in a contest he had initiated for the improvement of pronunciation. (See the later chapter: The Teacher). And it was while doing some research in the music archives of the National Theatre that he and one of his pupils came across six, hitherto unknown, juvenile dramas by the nineteenth century composer Ferenc Erkel—a discovery that led him to recognize Erkel as a precursor in the task of "bringing music and the people closer together."

In view of his intensive and varied cultural activities, a number of Academicians proposed, in 1941, that Kodály should be elected as a Corresponding Member of the Department of Philology and Aesthetics of the Academy of Sciences, but the proposal failed to obtain the two-third majority required at their meeting on 13th May. Meanwhile, Kodály was devoting increasing attention to a new periodical, *Singing Youth*, which had been founded by some of his pupils with the aim of promoting musical education amongst young people. In an introductory article he said that the journal would seek to "get rid of two kinds of musical illiteracy," by teaching people on the one hand to read music and on the other to appreciate true musical values. And in an interview with one of the papers he declared that "The foundations of a genuinely national musical consciousness have to be unearthed from beneath the accumulated rubble of Hungarian indifference and a misconceived and outmoded method of training. This is the spirit in which *Singing Youth* has been launched. Our movement rejects all distinctions based on class or social status. Music belongs to all." The full significance of these words, spoken in time of war, in a country that was rapidly drifting into fascism, can now be appreciated, for to-day the slogan "Music belongs to all" is rapidly being realized in practice. Nor did Kodály rely only on articles and lectures in his drive for musical education. More and more of his compositions were at this time directed to the same end: for example, *15 Two Part Exercises, Let us Sing Correctly, Bicinia Hungarica,* Volumes II—IV, *333 Reading Excercises,* and the two volumes of *Songs for Schools.*

In August 1942, having completed his thirty-five years of service, Kodály asked to be retired. But if the speed with which the Minister acceded to his request was an indication of the continued hostility of Hungarian officialdom, the people as a whole prepared to celebrate his sixtieth birthday in a variety of ways. The National Federation of Choral Societies proclaimed 1942 a 'Kodály Year'; the Ethnographical Society devoted a memorial volume to his work; and most of the musical periodicals published special issues. He was presented with the freedom of the city of Galánta, and Kolozsvár[20] conferred upon him an honorary degree; while a succession of concerts, devoted to his works, were organized throughout the country and abroad, the most important of these being the concert given by the Municipal Orchestra of Budapest, on 6th February, 1943, at which Kodály himself conducted the first European performance of his *Concerto,* and those of 24th February in Paris and of 10th June in Vienna. Moreover, the Academy of Sciences made amends for its rejection of him two years earlier, when, on 14th May, 1943, its General Assembly elected him, by thirty-five votes to eight, a Corresponding Member; and shortly afterwards to the Philological Committee, in which he played an active part.

The supreme achievement of these difficult years was the great *Missa Brevis,* which he dedicated to his wife. Originally written for the organ, later expanded by the addition of a mixed chorus, and finally fully orchestrated, this work bears all the marks of the force and maturity characteristic of Kodály's later style. In addition, in the two years 1943-44, he wrote ten new choruses, several of them settings to poems by Petőfi,[21] including *The Son of an*

Enslaved Country and *Still, by a Miracle, our Country Stands*—a choice that bears witness to Kodály's courage. In that hour of darkness, the century-old words—"The day of judgement still shall come, And loose our country from its chains"—rang out to Kodály's accompaniment like a clarion call.

Then, having uttered his artistic Credo, all creative activity was temporarily brought to a standstill by the German occupation. Not content with having forced Hungary into the suicidal action of taking part in the war against the Soviet Union, Hitler now vented his dissatisfaction with the support the Government was giving him by sacrificing every vital interest of the country; and when popular discontent at the useless expenditure of life rose to the point where even the Government was infected with the idea of concluding a separate peace, he sought to forestall such a contingency by occupying the country on 19th March, 1944, thus dooming her to certain destruction.

At first, Kodály retired to his flat in Buda to await the inevitable end of the war. Yet even during the height of the terror conducted by the Arrow-Cross Party[22] he continued to make daily journeys to the centre of the city, defying the air-raids and at the constant risk of his life, in order to do what he could to succour those who were being persecuted. Despite the insistent appeals of his friends, he refused to leave his suburban home, until eventually a gang of armed fascists forced their way in, and he only managed to save his wife and himself by his courage and presence of mind. For a while they found refuge in the air-raid shelter of a Convent in Próféta Street. And here, with fighting going on in the neighbouring streets, Kodály once more began to work, composing his chorus for female voices, *For Saint Agnes's Day*, in memory of the Mother Superior, who had, perhaps, been responsible for saving their lives.

By the end of 1944 the advancing Soviet Army had completely surrounded Budapest, but instead of accepting the Russian offer of surrender and thus saving the city unnecessary bloodshed and destruction, the Nazis and their Hungarian accomplices not only refused it but also shot the Soviet officers who were carrying the flag of truce. Thus began the siege. For weeks, in some districts for months, while the Soviet troops were overcoming the desperate resistance of the Nazis in house-to-house fighting, the population carried on their existence in underground shelters, starving and bitterly cold. Kodály and his wife left the Convent for the air-raid shelter at the Opera, where they spent the first months of 1945; and where, too, the *Missa Brevis* was performed for the first time, in a cloak-room transformed for the occasion into a concert hall.

At last, however, though the city lay in ruins, people once again began to breathe the air of freedom, leaving the darkness of their cellars behind them and turning their faces towards a peaceful future, striving to build a new life, while still mourning their dead. Kodály, having paid tribute to the victims of the war in *At the Grave of the Martyrs*, written for mixed choir and orchestra, turned once again to the future and to youth with his *24 Little Canons on the Black Keys*, the hundred folk songs in the first volume of *Pentatonic Music*, and the twelve short piano pieces, *Children's Dances*. As early as February 1945 he was elected President of the newly formed Arts Council, consisting of prominent representatives of all the fine and applied arts, which, in addition to assisting needy artists, gradually acquired a decisive authority in all matters relating to the development of the arts. By the end of the year, in addition to accepting the Presidency of the Musicians' Union and the chairmanship of the Board of Directors of the Academy of Music, he had been unanimously elected to membership of the Academy of Sciences and, in November, was chosen by the National Assembly to sit in Parliament as a distinguished artist and representative public figure.

Meanwhile, with his wife, Kodály spent a few months at Pécs and Dombóvár, recuperating from the strain and lack of food during the siege, though this did not prevent him from giving several lectures and discussing their problems with the local teachers of music. In the following spring, at a Memorial Concert for his friend Bartók, who had died suddenly in America in tragic circumstances, after paying a glowing tribute to the great composer's music, he went on to castigate the low level of musical culture in his country for having created a barrier between Bartók's work and the public. In July, in the course of a lecture to the Congress of the Hungarian—Soviet Friendship Society, he declared: "The idea that the common people also have a contribution to make in the field of culture was expressed for the first time during the intellectual ferment that preceded the French Revolution... It is a source of great encouragement that to-day, for the first time, the common people of Hungary are entering this field, not only as consumers, but also as producers. What we have to learn from the Soviet Union is, first and foremost, to appreciate art and the artist as they deserve." And later in the month, in his inaugural address as President of the General Assembly of the Academy of Sciences, he expressed the view that his one qualification for the position was "the esteem in which I hold both the main departments of the Academy (the humanities and the sciences), which to-day sometimes find themselves in opposition. If I should succeed in producing harmony by instilling both departments with a true respect for the other, I should be satisfied that I had fulfilled my task."

In October 1946, interrupting this succession of public activities, Kodály visited Britain and the United States, travelling with his wife *via* Switzerland and France. At a number of concerts, many of them conducted by himself, his music was acclaimed, particularly the *Háry János Suite*, the *Dances of Galánta* and the *Missa Brevis*. On his return, after a few days' rest, he set off on another tour, this time to the Soviet Union, where he conducted concerts of his work both in Moscow and in Leningrad, the last two movements of the *Háry János Suite*, played by the Leningrad Philharmonic, being twice encored.

Speaking of his experience during this latter tour to a meeting of the Academy, he emphasized the importance of the encouragement given to cultural work by the Soviet authorities. "The way the Soviet State provides for its scientists and artists," he said, "removing every obstacle from their path, should be an example to any country which regards the promotion of culture as being one of the functions of Government. And all that the Soviet State demands in return is that its scientists and artists should dedicate themselves to their work. This is another respect in which the model she offers deserves to be copied." And in an interview with *Die Brücke*, the journal of the Austrian-Soviet Cultural Society, he praised the exemplary organization of musical training in the Soviet Union.

Once again, as five years previously, Kodály's birthday was widely celebrated by music-lovers, but now, at sixty-five, there were official honours as well. In addition to receiving the freedom of his native town, Kecskemét, he was invested with the Grand Cross of the Order of the Republic by the Minister of Education; and on 15th March, 1948, he was one of the first of his countrymen to be awarded the newly instituted Kossuth Prize, "for signal services in the fields of science and the arts." On the same evening his new opera, *Czinka Panna*, written to a libretto by Béla Balázs,[23] was given for the first time by the Budapest Opera Company. Though the opera did not meet with the success that was expected, due to the historical distortions of the libretto, the critics' only complaint of the music was that there was too little of it; and indeed there are parts of it—notably the *Minuetto Serio* and the *Rákóczi March*—that brilliantly evoke the spirit of the anti-Habsburg war of independence in the 18th century.

In spite of a number of trips abroad during the course of the year, conducting concerts of his works in Stockholm, Vienna and England, and of presiding over the jury at the International Bartók Festival of Modern Music in Budapest, Kodály still found time to compose a number of new works. Many of these were arrangements for choirs, including the five variations on the Marseillaise, which he called *A Hymn to Liberty*, and the fine setting of the *Fiftieth Geneva Psalm*, in which he used the Hungarian version of Albert Szenczi Molnár.[24] And, finally, as the result of an anonymous competition, he and Jenő Ádám were commissioned to edit a new series of song-books for use in the primary schools.

Yet, despite his almost universal prestige, he was unable to prevent the triumph of principles diametrically opposed to his own at the Academy of Music. Training in solfeggio, the introduction of which had been one of his greatest achievements, was abolished, and the Faculty of School Music was dissolved. Nor was his task as President of the Academy of Sciences an easy one. It soon became clear that the organizational structure and methods of that venerable institution were inadequate to the new requirements, and that a number of drastic reforms were necessary. Kodály not only contributed a number of suggestions in this respect, but did much to promote the work of the Committee that was set up to draft a new Constitution. When his three-year term of office expired, there were good grounds for the gratitude expressed by the Secretary General "for the care and circumspection with which you have carried out the duties of your office... for your courageous stand in support of the Academy's interests, and for the straightforward way in which you have drawn our attention to existing shortcomings." Yet though relinquishing office was a welcome release from often burdensome functions, he continued to play an important part in the reorganized institution; and in 1949 the preparation of the *Thesaurus of Hungarian Folk Music* for the press was resumed after an interruption of many years, with Kodály in charge of the work.

The next two years, after being elected Honorary President of the newly formed Association of Musicians in October 1949, he spent on another long trip to France and Britain, where he again conducted his own works, and on visiting a number of towns in Hungary for the purpose of promoting musical education. And at a memorial concert at the Budapest Opera on the fifth anniversary of Bartók's death, speaking of the dead composer, he said: "He belonged to that order of human beings, who, for ever dissatisfied, feel impelled to transform everything, to improve the quality of whatever is to be found on earth... Naturally, there are plenty of people who would like to change the world, but lack the power to do so. Bartók had that power. For there is in his music that mysterious, living and life-giving force that the work of many other composers, though outwardly similar, essentially lacks."

For Kodály, the climax of 1950 came on 25th November, in Zurich, when Victor Reinshagen conducted a full version of *Háry János*, in a magnificent production that fascinated the audience with the strange beauty of the work. But, unfortunately, what would have been a great triumph was brought to an abrupt end by the death of the leading singer, the superb Endre Böhm. Now, once again as in 1924, the composer turned to Bach, in his *Three Choral Preludes* transcribing the *Chromatic Fantasy* for viola, and the *Prelude and Fugue in E flat Minor* for 'cello and piano. And in the same period he added to his choral works, with the *Kálló Folk Dances for Chorus and Orchestra*, the *Hundred-and-Fourteenth Geneva Psalm*, and his setting of a poem by Sándor Weöres, *A Song for Peace*.

At the same time, in addition to his work at the Academy of Music, he continued to be active in the Academy of Sciences, whose Committee of Musicology elected him as Chairman in September 1951. While, before the year was out, the first volume of the *Thesaurus of Hungarian Folk Music, Children's Games*, was published, with a short introduction in which Kodály summed up its significance; and his fight for the re-introduction of solfeggio training at the Academy was at last successful.

In 1952, to celebrate his own seventieth birthday and the seventieth anniversary of the death of the great poet, Arany,[25] he published, in conjunction with Ágost Gyulai, *The Folk-Song Collection of János Arany*. Throughout the year he was showered with honours by the Government and learned societies. In addition to receiving a second Kossuth Prize, he was awarded the First Division of the Order of the Hungarian People's Republic, and the title of "Eminent Artist." The Institute of Cultural Relations with Foreign Countries published a volume of his essays and articles devoted to his work in English, Russian, German and French; and a Memorial Volume, edited by Bence Szabolcsi and Dénes Bartha, was issued by the Academy of Sciences. A particularly charming tribute was paid to him at a meeting of the Ethnographical Society, when Mrs. Márta Lőrincz, a Székely repatriate, who forty years earlier had sung for him when he was collecting folk songs in her village, greeted him with a folk tune that had not previously been recorded.

Meanwhile, in a variety of forms—articles, essays, lectures and newspaper polemics—his educational activities continued, culminating in the publication of his *33, 44* and *55 Two-Part Singing Exercises*, and the twenty-eight minor pieces of the *Tricinia*, dedicated to "the better musicians of our better future." For awhile, in 1954, they were abated somewhat by an unfortunate accident to his wife, as a result of which she was obliged to spend several months in hospital. But no sooner had she recovered than he resumed his energetic public life. In 1955 he spoke twice on the radio, and delivered a lecture at the Academy of Sciences "From Szentirmay[26] to Bartók"; and on the tenth anniversary of the latter's death, he accepted the chairmanship of the Bartók Memorial Committee, and later of the Mozart Committee. And all the time he was continuing to write music: in 1955 the major *a cappella* work, *Zrínyi's Appeal*, for baritone solo and chorus, and (at the request of the People's Army Ensemble) an accompaniment to Petőfi's *National Ode*; and, in 1956, a number of choral works—settings of three poems by M. Vörösmarty, and a transcription of the Intermezzo from *Háry*, with words by Károly Vargha.

From 22nd October, 1956 to 8th January, 1957 he and Mrs. Kodály were staying at Galyatető, a mountain resort in the north of the country, so that they were absent from Budapest at the time of the counter-revolutionary rising. On his return, he was awarded a Kossuth Prize for the third time, and in the following July he was elected President of the Music Council, newly set up by the Ministry of Education. But all too soon the celebrations that greeted his seventy-fifth birthday were succeeded by mourning, for on 22nd November, 1958, in the forty-ninth year of their marriage, Emma Kodály died. What her death meant to him may be best expressed in his own words of leave-taking: "In the course of her life she was a blessing to everyone who met her. Wherever her bright eyes rested there was light and warmth and life, for they radiated an infinite kindness. To-day she is being mourned by every man and woman who has felt even a little of the warmth of her loving heart, but how much more by him upon whom she lavished the fulness of her gifts, and whose life she made a paradise upon earth." It had been her wish that, when she died, he should not remain lonely and uncared-for, but should find a companion who would bring into his hard-working life the loving kindness she could no longer give him. Such a companion he was to find in Sarolta Péczely, a student at the Faculty of Conductors at the Academy, whom he was to marry a year later, in December 1959. Thanks to her loving care, the ageing master is still able to pursue his manifold activities both in Hungary and abroad. In 1960, at the age of seventy-seven, he was conducting his own music in Britain, lectured at Oxford University on the occasion of his receiving an honorary degree, and was invited, in the company of Britten, Shaporin and Poulenc, to write a new choral work to a passage from *The Merchant of Venice*. To-day, when the whole world pays homage to his music, the words he once spoke of Bartók are equally true of himself: "Every time one of his works is performed people will be reminded of his native Hungary and, if nothing else, they will say to themselves, 'A nation that can produce such music cannot be without worth.'"

THE MUSICOLOGIST

It is often supposed that, between the scholar and the artist, there exists some essential incompatibility of function and temperament, yet Kodály is a living refutation of this view. As he himself has said, in an address to the Academy of Sciences: "Not only is there a close relation between the various sciences... but it is also true that science and art cannot do without one another. The more of the artist there is in the scientist the more fitted is he for his calling, and *vice versa*. Lacking intuition and imagination, the work of a scientist will at best be pedestrian; without a sense of inner order, of constructive logic, the artist will remain on the periphery of art." From this point of view Kodály was well equipped by his early training. The habit of scholarship, acquired at the University and Eötvös College, has continued throughout his life, particularly in the two fields of folklore and musical criticism; and so important are the results of his study that both fields must be considered more closely.

Scholar and Folklorist

Kodály's determination to become a collector of folk songs was no sudden inspiration: it matured slowly. Already while living at Galánta he had become attached to the peasantry and their music, and as a student at Nagyszombat he had been interested in such collections of folk songs as then existed. In 1896 he first came across the name Béla Vikár, the first man to use the phonograph for recording folk songs; and it was from him, seven years later, that he was to learn how to use the wax cylinder. By that time Kodály had compared the printed versions of the songs with the phonograph recordings in the Ethnographical Museum, and found that the former had been deliberately modified, in such a way that their essentially Magyar characteristics were lost. And it was this that set him upon the path of collecting folk songs himself, for he realized that it was only in the villages that he could hope to find the genuine, unadulterated music.

It was in 1905 that he reached this conclusion, and he has described the occasion: "Knapsack on back and stick in hand, and with fifty crowns in my pocket, I set out for the Csallóköz, intending to roam about the countryside without any very definite plan. Sometimes I would just buttonhole people in the street, invite them to come and have a drink and get them to sing for me; or sometimes I would listen to the women singing as they worked at the harvest. But the most exhausting part was the nightly sessions in the smoky atmosphere of the village pubs." Galánta was the starting-point of this first tour. There he began by getting his old school-mates to sing the songs he remembered from childhood, going on to visit some dozen villages, and calling on former servants of the family and their relatives.

At the end of a month he had collected one hundred and fifty songs, fifteen of which he published in *Ethnographia*, under the title "Songs from Mátyusföld." Thus, when working on his diploma thesis, "The Stanzaic Structure of Hungarian Folk Song," he was able to make use of his own research as well as earlier published sources. To-day, in the light of more recent work—partly by Kodály himself—some of the views he then expressed have had to be modified, but in essentials the conclusions he then reached remain valid. "Folk song," he wrote, "is essentially vocal, it lives only in song. Without the melody, the words are incomplete; and, of the two con-stituents, the melody, the older and more permanent, is the more important. . . It is impossible to study folk songs satisfactorily, particularly to investigate their rhythms, unless one hears them actually performed. Moreover, however extensive our knowledge and experience may be, it is only through hearing them sung by the peasants themselves that we can be certain as to their correct interpretation."

Having completed his thesis he became a member of the Ethnographical Society, and, in each of the next ten years, as a result of a new collecting tour, he published a paper in the society's journal. For the most part these are unpretentious reports of the material he had collected and recorded, but their importance was pointed out many years later, in 1952, by Kodály himself. In the Preface to Volume II of *The Thesaurus of Hungarian Folk Music*, he wrote: "The elaboration of theories based on the evidence of inadequate and unreliable material was common practice amongst the scientists of the old Hungary. They regarded the reliability of their source material as of secondary importance, so that many of their faulty texts have had to be revised. With the discovery of a single new fact the most brilliant theory may well collapse like a house of cards. Theories will often become obsolete; correctly recorded material, never."

For this reason it was fortunate that so great a part in the collection of folk music should have been played by Kodály and Bartók, two men in whom the artist's intuition was combined with the scholar's capacity for

Béla Bartók in 1902
(At the time of his first meeting with Kodály)

A Page from one of the Notebooks (1906) in which Kodály
Recorded Folk Songs)

classification. Believing that the purest folk music was to be found in the border regions[27]—a belief that proved to be well-founded—Kodály suggested that their first tour should concentrate on these areas. As he recalled later: "We divided up the district to be explored according to a plan. Then from time to time we would meet in order to compare our material, and pool our written records of the songs." Until they could afford to buy their own apparatus they borrowed recording phonographs from the Ethnographical Society, finding these essential for their work, not merely on account of the faithful record they produced, but also because an instrument that could immediately play back a song that had just been sung acted as a helpful stimulus to the peasant singers. They soon found that the old people were the best exponents of folk music, the younger generation being more attracted to fashionable popular songs. "On the whole," as Kodály was to note, "though it varied from place to place, we were to find the peasants more sympathetic to our undertaking than the rural intelligentzia... Only the school-teachers really grasped what we were about, and they for the most part were helpful... Of course, there were occasions when we were received with suspicion, for the peasants had been so often tricked by town's people that they were apt to distrust a well-dressed stranger. It wasn't so bad as long as we went on foot, but when we needed a carriage to take all our equipment they smelt a rat, suspecting some kind of 'business'... One obstacle we encountered was that the old people, whom we were most anxious to record, were not only shy of the young folk, but were also debarred by village etiquette from singing in public. Another difficulty was persuading women to sing, except on the sly, because it was generally held that women only sang in public if they were drunk. The men, however, were ready enough to co-operate, once they had had a glass or two. But much the most favourable times for the collector were such joint activities as a husking-bee or feather-plucking, when the peasants sang naturally at their work."

Obviously, therefore, the task the two friends had set themselves was a strenuous one. Moreover, since in Government circles there was little appreciation of the cultural value of what they were doing, as well as marked hostility to the peasants, no financial support was officially forthcoming. Thus, for a long time, this important research work remained the private concern of these two men, financed, at considerable cost to themselves, by what they could save from their salaries. Later, however, as their collection accumulated, the cost of arranging and publishing it, which had become imperative, proved to be beyond their means, and they therefore drafted 'A Plan for the New Universal Collection of Folk Songs,' in the hope that the Kisfaludy Society might be induced to support it.

4

After pointing to the serious lack of "any full and systematic publication of folk music," which they attributed mainly to the mistake of over-valuing the words at the expense of the tunes, they went on to stress the point, already made by Kodály in his thesis, that the true and essential characteristics of the songs "only become intelligible if it is realized that they were created to be sung, not to be recited." They therefore urged the importance of preparing "the fullest possible, most accurate and strictly critical edition of Hungarian folk songs, and other folk music, which would constitute an authoritative 'Corpus Musicae Popularis.'" The backbone of such a work, they suggested, should be "our collection, which already covers most of the ethnographically interesting regions of Hungary, and comprises some 3,000 tunes with words, as well as 100 examples of instrumental music for bagpipes, flute or violin." These, together with such examples from previous collections as survived critical examination, the phonograph recordings by Béla Vikár, and transcripts by various of Kodály's students and collaborators, would amount to between 5,000 and 6,000 items—"a figure," as they cautiously observed, "signifying a degree of completeness, since there is hardly a district of importance that would not be represented by a number of tunes."

An important section of the Draft expounds the method of presentation they proposed to follow. "Hitherto, publication of folk music has either been quite unsystematic, or based on classification by the words of the songs... Thanks to the development of comparative musicology, however, the only satisfactory arrangement is one based on the characteristics of the music, so that the principal types will clearly emerge from the various groups of tunes of kindred derivation. Only an arrangement on these lines can provide easy reference, and a simple method of collating and comparing one collection with another. The best example of this method is to be found in the collections of songs recently published by the Finnish Literary Society... The essence of this method, which we ourselves have followed, is that all tunes have been reduced to a common terminal note, i. e. have been transcribed so that they end on G. flat Since, with few exceptions, the tunes consist of four lines, three line-endings have to be considered, the most important being the second, which concludes the first half of the song. All tunes whose second line ends on the same note are classified as belonging to a single group; the groups thus constituted are then broken down into sub-groups, according to the final note of the first line; and these again are yet further sub-divided according to the final note of the third line. Integrated with this method of classification is another, based on rhythm, by which the tunes are grouped in order of length; and within these groups the tunes are further arranged according to register, proceeding from the shortest to the longest... Instru-

50

mental music would be confined to an Appendix, since this consists in the main of longer pieces, which do not fit into the above arrangement."

As each volume was to contain about 1,000 tunes, the whole work would have comprised five or six volumes, with a seventh devoted to indexes and notes. Aware of the importance of indexes for serious study, they were of the opinion that these should include: "1. Two textual indexes, one of opening lines, another of subjects, of the songs; 2. An index of place names, with page references to the songs belonging to them; 3. An index of themes; 4. An index of sources; 5. An index of words sung to more than one tune, and of songs with alternative words. And, finally, 6. A full bibliography of each song."

From the above it is clear that, right at the beginning of their work, the two men had given considerable thought to methodology. Later, Bartók was to adopt a different principle. In his book, *The Hungarian Folk Song* (1924), he divided his material into three groups: A. consisting of the oldest songs; B. the more recent ones; and C. those which, from the stylistic point of view, did not fit into either of the others. The purpose of this was to distinguish the two dominant and most characteristic styles of Hungarian folk song, in order to treat them individually. But his aim was fully realized only in respect of Group B, for in separating Groups A and C he introduced a further principle, classifying all isometrical tunes as A, and all hetero-metrical ones as C. The result of this was to exclude a number of the older tunes from Group A, while admitting many others that, on grounds of structure and tonality, were alien to it.

Naturally, in the fifty years since the inception of the undertaking, the method of arrangement has made many advances, partly due to scientific developments, but partly, also, as a result of the ten-fold increase in the number of songs thanks to the subsidizing of research by the State. Moreover, Kodály has modified the view he held in 1913, and now considers that the best method of classification is one which takes into account the content as well as the formal criteria. In this he has been followed by the Folk Music Research Group of the Academy of Sciences, which, since 1951, has been responsible for editing volume after volume of *The Thesaurus of Hungarian Folk Music*. The material so far published is classified according to either the words or the functional purpose of the songs, e. g. Children's Games, Songs for Red-Letter Days, for Weddings or Betrothals, or Funeral Dirges. In the volumes yet to be published, where the tunes are not functional, they will be arranged on musical grounds. The purpose of this method is to bring together all variants of kindred types of song, so that every type and style of folk music will be represented, while at the same time providing an easy means of reference. Since this principle of classification depends primarily on the relation between the opening and closing lines, it is distinguished from the earlier one only in so far as it does not make cadence the sole criterion. Like Bartók's system, it segregates the older and more recent styles, while doing away with his unsatisfactory Group C, so that this new arrangement is seen to be a synthesis of, rather than a compromise between, the principles employed by Bartók and Kodály.

Such, briefly, is the history of five decades of folk-song methodology. We must now return to an earlier stage in Kodály's career as a musicologist. Having completed the Draft Plan with Bartók, and after publishing one or two polemical articles, a new phase in his scientific work, of cardinal importance for the development of research, opened in 1917 with the first of a series of articles, "The Pentatonic Scale in Hungarian Folk Music." In a prefatory note he said: "That the pentatonic scale—the origin of music for so many, perhaps for all, peoples—is still alive and flourishing in this country, has been known since 1907, when for the first time Béla Bartók discovered a large group of such songs in the Székely region." Then, after drawing attention to the wide dispersal of this type of music, in Transylvania and Bucovina, as well as western Hungary and amongst the Hungarian-speaking population of what is now Slovakia, he proceeded to make a careful analysis of the songs from the point of view of tempo, rhythm and structure. Basing himself on the scores of a number of songs from Bartók's and other collections, he was able to show for the first time that the pentatonic scale, without semi-tones and in a minor key, is the main characteristic of Magyar melodies. And he modestly concluded: "Full investigation must wait until we have a substantial and representative collection of songs. Until then, any theory is unavoidably built on sand. For us, to-day, there is only one thing to be done: we must gather in the harvest before it perishes in the field. The sole purpose of what I have written is to stress that there are still territories in Hungary awaiting exploration."

In his next essay of importance, "The Song of Argirus" (1920)[28], Kodály investigated the ancient Hungarian romances. "For the man of the 20th century," he observed, "a poem is something to be read. Only the peasant lives at the same level as the ancient Greeks, for whom words and music were an indivisible unity. Originally the music was an essential component, not only of the lyric, but also of the epic, for we know that epic poetry from Homer to the Kalevala was sung." That the old Hungarian romances, these centuries-old rhymed tales, were sung, is no mere conjecture. For it is known that Sebestyén Tinódi, "the lute player," a notable 16th century author of romances and rhymed chronicles, also wrote the music for them. Furthermore, as Kodály pointed out, "the romances have certain stylistic peculiarities which, if the music is ignored, can no more be understood than can those of old lyrics or of folk songs. Dissemination of the romances was by word-of-mouth; and, insofar as they have been traditionally preserved, it is always in association with the tune. Though printing has contributed to their survival, the tradition has been mainly oral, the sung words being passed on from generation to generation." Kodály had himself heard one of these romances, the "Song of Argirus," still being sung by the peasants of Bucovina in the spring of 1914, and by a detailed analysis of the tune he had then recorded he was able to expose certain mistakes in earlier printed versions of the song, in which only the words had been preserved. Basing himself on János Horváth's[29] work on the history of prosody, he arrived at two conclusions: "Firstly, when investigating any type of song the first question one must ask is: Is there a tune for it? Was it ever sung, or was it only to be read? It is an illusion to suppose that the real significance of a song can be appreciated merely through its rhythm, if its tune is left out. Secondly, anyone wishing to achieve a proper understanding of our ancient prosody must be equipped with all the lessons that are to be learned from the study of folk song, in which words and music live side by side."

In a minor essay he wrote in 1923, "The Evolution of Musical Folklore," Kodály examined the reasons for the contemporary interest in folk music, and concluded that it arose from three main causes. "One factor," he wrote, "is the endeavour to establish a national musical style; another is the contemporary interest in all exotic music; and the third is the development of comparative musicology. In some countries, the desire for self-realization, the urge to get at the roots of the national spirit, has excited the curiosity of certain composers to such an extent that they have felt impelled to seek out the national musical heritage still preserved in the countryside. It was the Spaniard, Eximeno, who, in the 18th century, formulated, perhaps for the first time, the idea that the art music of every country ought to be based on its folk music—an idea that bore fruit in the multitude of national styles that evolved in the course of the 19th century." And he went on to point out that, despite the rapidly growing accumulation of recorded music, its publication, originally interrupted by the war, was still being held up. No headway had been made with the proposed *Thesaurus of Hungarian Folk Music*. All that had appeared were the two slim volumes, *The Hungarians of Transylvania (Folk Songs)*, and *The Collection of Nagyszalonta*, containing a total of 192 tunes, mostly the result of the researches of Kodály and Bartók.

An essay published in 1926, though it had been written in 1918, "Clement the Mason,"[30] is interesting for two reasons: Kodály's notes on the best methods of collecting, and the very detailed transcription of the score of the ballad. The collector, he considers, should preferably be a combination of musician and folklorist, and it is advisable to use a phonographic recorder, "especially when it is a case of recording improvisations which can never be exactly repeated," for example, funeral dirges, or keening songs. "The phonograph also facilitates the study of highly melismatic music," he says, "for by slowing down the machine when playing back it is possible to observe the details or ornamentation as it were through a microscope." He follows this with the score of the hitherto unknown ballad, which had been discovered in Transylvania, transcribing the variants one below the other so that the minutest differences may be easily observed.

The time was now approaching when, after a vast amount of research, it was becoming necessary to attempt some evaluation of the results. Kodály's first essay in this direction was the article "Hungarian Folk Music" already referred to, that he contributed in 1931 to the *Encyclopaedia of Music*. Here he set out to do two things: on the one hand, to provide a concise historical survey of the various types of folk music, illustrated by 25 specimen scores; and, on the other, to distinguish clearly between genuine, and pseudo folk music, or what he called "urban folk songs." This was all the more necessary because, particularly in the latter half of the 19th century, a tremendous amount of this pseudo folk music had been *composed*, and published, in Hungary.

A more comprehensive work was the paper, "Ethnography and Musical History," which, first delivered as a lecture, was subsequently printed in *Ethnographia*. Beginning with a short history of ethnographical studies in Hungary, and ruefully contrasting the position there with the much greater volume of such work available in Switzerland or England, he goes on to point out that in Hungary secular music only began to be written down in the 16th century, and that it was not until the end of the 18th that this became the regular practice. As a result, as he puts it, "the tradition of secular music in our country is like an underground river: only part of its course is visible." Such written music as has survived is far from presenting a complete picture of our musical heritage, for, as in most ancient and oriental cultures, far the greater part has been handed down to us by oral tradition. It was only with the spread of polyphonic music that the need for written scores arose, and polyphony had flourished for several centuries in the rest of Europe before it made headway in Hungary, so that even in the 20th century our musical culture relies as much on oral tradition as on written music. "However," comments Kodály, "this signifies a distinction not of quality, but only of age... As a nation, we were born later than most other

54

European nations... But youth has its advantages, and it may well be that we shall still have something to say when other nations have spoken their last word."

He then proceeds to collate the manuscripts and printed texts of a number of songs with the versions that have survived in oral tradition, and points out that in almost every case the written version has preserved little more than the skeleton of the living music. From this he concludes that true folk music "not only has never been written down, but cannot be adequately recorded in writing... A scientifically valid study of it can only be made by hearing it performed *viva voce*... Our starting-point, therefore, must be the living reality, the reality which, despite the difficulties, we can still discover to-day. Only then should we set out on our slow and cautious journey into the receding past. Few ancient scores are still extant, but instead of grieving for what we haven't got we should rejoice all the more in what we still have. We should take pride in the fact that we belong to a nation that still has a living tradition; that the more valuable part of our musical heritage, instead of mouldering away in libraries, is abundantly alive; that we are privileged to be able to experience at first hand a stage of development that the peoples of the West can only know by reconstructing it." And he gives this warning: "A scientific understanding of folk music is a necessary precondition for any serious work on the history of Hungarian music. Only with such knowledge can we invest the cold facts of that history with the colours and warmth of life... In Hungary, no one who has failed to absorb our living musical tradition and to develop it in his own way can be either a creative composer or a creative musicologist. Not only our musical life, but our whole culture, has been split into two worlds that scarcely ever communicate. On the one side is our higher culture, borrowed, transplanted and nourished from foreign sources; on the other, our popular culture, firmly rooted in tradition... Only when these two are brought together can there be real life. In countries with a happier history, their higher culture is a direct continuation of the popular culture. But we have been robbed of that possibility. For us, the first essential is that those who are responsible for transmitting this higher culture must also assimilate our popular culture, so that it is transformed into an integral and harmonious part of their own education. This higher culture, imported from abroad, will only bear fruit if it strikes roots deep in the culture of the people. Only when the contradictions that still separate our native traditions and our imported cultural institutions have gradually died away, and when these institutions have learnt to foster our traditions and develop them in accordance with their natural growth, only then will the dream of an integrated Hungarian culture, which to-day exists only in the imagination of a few, become a reality for all." These are the words of both scholar and educationalist, striving to awaken the conscience of the intelligentsia and to inspire them with a noble aim. But in the next of his essays to be published, "The Distinctive Melodic Structure of Cheremiss Folk Music" (1934), it was once again the single-minded scholar who was speaking, drawing attention to the close similarity that exists between Hungarian and Cheremiss, or Mari, folk songs. "It seems likely," he concludes, "that the more we familiarize ourselves with the music of kindred peoples in the East, the more connections shall we discover between it and our own"; and he therefore urged that an early start should be made in the scientific collection of the songs from these regions.

Then, in 1937, after thirty-two years of active research and hard scientific thinking, his outstanding work on the subject, *The Folk Music of Hungary*, was at last published. This, though in size little more than a monograph, is not only the most comprehensive treatment of the whole of the material available, but is also the most significant achievement of a Hungarian musicologist and a remarkable contribution to the history of our culture as a whole. As Dénes Bartha has truly said of it: "By exploring the sources and origins of the various types of Hungarian folk song, Kodály has performed an entirely novel scientific work. From our knowledge of the extensive literature in this field, we can assert without exaggeration that there is no scholar in Europe so profoundly familiar as he with the musical heritage both of Europe and of Asia." The study, which has subsequently been translated into German, Russian and English, devotes a separate chapter to each of the following themes: the popular musical tradition, the primitive stratum of folk music, later developments in folk songs, songs for children, minstrel's lays, and dirges or keening songs; and it then goes on to discuss the reciprocal influences between folk music and written, or art music, and the important question of the relation of popular tradition to musical culture as a whole.

In a much shorter essay, he then sets out to provide an answer to the question, "What is the Hungarian Spirit in Music?" It is to be found above all, he suggests, in the most primitive layers of Hungarian folk music. "Like our language," he says, "our music is laconic and lapidary: a series of masterpieces, small in size but of great weight; themes consisting of few notes, which, as though they had been carved in stone, have weathered the storms of centuries. There is such finality about their form that they have not changed in a thousand years; and in some cases their exact counterparts have been discovered amongst kindred peoples, as though it were only yesterday that they had ceased singing them together... Broadly speaking, Hungarian music is active rather than passive, an expression of the will rather than of the feelings. It is remote from self-indulgent grief, from 'delight in tears.'[31] Even the Székely 'laments' are infused with energy and determination... Its rhythms are trenchant, sharply defined and varied. Its melodies do not emerge timidly from a preconceived harmonic base, but are dynamic and free-flowing. Its forms are concise, well-proportioned, and transparently clear... The Magyar spirit is more akin to the Greco-Roman sense of form than to the Nordic mists." Then, after pointing out that every important national school of music is the result of an intermixture of different civilizations and races, and that this is particularly true of Hungary, he concludes: "A nation living at the meeting point of East and West must inevitably strive to belong to both, seeking to reconcile and dissolve their conflicts in itself... The greater our stake in the culture of Europe the greater will our own become... Isolated from that culture, our national characteristics will merely atrophy."

The argument summarized in this article (which was published in three journals, including the English-language *Hungarian Quarterly*, in 1940) was developed in greater detail by Kodály in the essay, "The Hungarian Element in Music," which he contributed to a volume called *What is Hungarian?* that came out in 1939. After drawing attention to the main characteristics of Hungarian folk music—the accented opening, the falling melodic line, and the pentatonic scale—he extends his enquiry beyond the purely musical aspects of the question and considers the social conditions and foreign influences that affect the creation of music. "In its emergent stage," he writes, "our own art music was subjected to two major German influences in the 19th century. These were iambic melody at the beginning, and Wagnerian opera at the end. To-day, we may be said to have recovered from both these influences, having learnt a great deal from them, though not without cost to ourselves." And the conclusion he reaches is the same as that in the earlier article: "While each separate element of Hungarian music is to be found in the music of other nations, nowhere else is there precisely this combination of them." What constitutes the specific colour and flavour of a national music is the interplay of native tradition and foreign influences.

The advances that had been made in the study of musical folklore, resulting from the work of Bartók and Kodály, had raised a number of new questions, some of which Kodály explored in his paper, "Folk Music and Art Music," published in 1941. In the preface he stresses the point that "in unilingual countries, when development has been unimpeded, both types of music are the product of the same spirit, for the same spirit exists both in the upper and lower levels of their culture. Their art music grows out of their folk music, the former emerging as an organic continuation, a refined and fuller development of the latter." But in Hungary such was not the case. There, "higher art music... when from time to time it did find expression, did not spring from the genius of the people, but was imported ready-made, and it remained what it had always been, an expression of the spirit of another nation." He then goes on to examine the stratification of musical culture in Hungary, and draws attention to the "very thin layer of musically educated people, completely absorbed in foreign masterpieces, mainly of Italian or German origin."[32] This advanced music was dismissed as unintelligible by the middle class, who much preferred the pseudo folk music composed for the gypsy orchestras. Both middle class and aristocracy looked upon the genuinely Hungarian music of the peasants as something of an oddity, since they considered that they themselves "had long since outgrown the primitive Ugric-Turkish culture of which it was an expression." What Kodály particularly condemned in the attitude of the middle class was the smug self-satisfaction with which they attributed their failure to appreciate either the best art music on the one hand, or folk music on the other, to their own robustly Hungarian outlook, whereas in fact "the real barrier to appreciation was, in the first case, their defective education, and, in the second, their ignorance of the true spirit of Hungary."

In a number of his writings, Kodály was concerned to show that the study of musical folklore was not, as was generally assumed, something entirely new in Hungary. In one essay, "Hungarian Musical Folklore a Century Ago," he describes the endeavour to form a collection of folk songs that had been made in 1832 by the Scientific Society, the predecessor of the Academy of Sciences, as well as Dániel Mindszenty's collection of eighty-eight folk songs; and discusses these early attempts at classification. In another, "Three Folk Tunes of Lukács Mihalovits," he makes a detailed analysis of these newly discovered and typical examples of early 19th century *verbunkos*, or soldiers' recruiting dances. He makes the point that, though musically insignificant, these pieces repay study, since "analysis reveals the almost chemical purity of the platitudes contained in them, thus enabling us to grasp the specific contribution that has been made by the greater musicians who have elaborated them." For the musicologist, he says, the exploration of antecedents is important because, "in order fully to appreciate a particular style, we must be able to trace it from its first emergence, through its maturity, to its decline, charting all its ramifications, and verifying the laws by which it is determined at each stage of its development... Thorough examination of the material must come first, and is the essential basis for further understanding. As we have seen all too often in our country, mere aestheticizing, over-intellectualizing without adequate first-hand experience, is merely building castles of sand." In yet a third essay falling within this group, "Hungarian Dances from 1729," which was written in 1952, he discusses six dance tunes that had recently been discovered in manuscript. Speaking of the responsibility of musicologists for the development of music, he urges them to work in such a way that composers will be able to concentrate on their art, instead of being obliged to divert their energies to scholarship. "In this way, he writes, musicology will come to transcend its professional limitations and play a significant part in our national culture, by purifying the national consciousness of our country and shaping its future."

The most important of Kodály's recent scientific works, however, is undoubtedly *The Folk-Song Collection of János Arany*, which, with Ágost Gyulai, he edited in 1952. The original manuscript contains 148 tunes—genuine folk songs as well as composed, pseudo folk songs—that the poet had recorded during his lifetime. In publishing this annotated edition, which also contains in an Appendix a number of tunes composed by Arany himself, Kodály was not motivated merely by a feeling of reverence for the great poet who had died seventy years earlier. As he insists, "it is a work of fundamental importance, which, had it been published in his lifetime, might have exerted considerable influence on the development both of music and of poetry; and which, we are convinced, will not be without its effect to-day." The collection is characteristic of the eighteen-thirties, a crucial phase in the development of folk song in Hungary, when the *biedermeyer* tendency was already driving a wedge between popular tradition and educated taste. And, as Kodály emphasizes, the result of this tendency was "to prevent the music of popular tradition from growing naturally into a higher style, thus setting back our musical development by a hundred years." As to the significance of the collection, this may perhaps best be summarized by quoting from a lecture on the same subject that Kodály subsequently delivered at the Academy of Sciences. It is important, he said, "Firstly, because it provides fresh and independent information that helps us to fill out the portrait we have of Arany... Secondly, it is a unique indication of the folk songs that were available in the eighteen-thirties... And thirdly, it reveals the musical basis of Arany's theoretical and practical investigations into prosody[33]... If he was able to derive inspiration for such poetry as his from a mere handful of songs like this, how much greater inspiration should the poets of our own day be able to discover in the huge collections now available... The time has arrived when folk song—not the words alone, but that indivisible unity of words and music—may well exert as great, maybe a greater, influence on our poetry than it did a century ago. And, if this should happen, it must lead to an undreamed-of revival of our metrical forms."

To attempt to give an account, even a brief summary, of all Kodály's musicological writings would be beyond the scope of this book. All we can hope to have achieved is to give some indication of the wide range of his interests, of his zest as a scholar, and of his brilliant and profound insight. As to the value of his achievement in this field, this was already appreciated by Bartók as long ago as 1921, when, speaking of Kodály in his article, "The New Music of Hungary," he said: "What musical folklore in Hungary owes to him is fully recognized by the experts. His zeal for research, his perseverance and thoroughness, his erudition and his perspicacity make him the one completely informed authority on Hungarian peasant music—a subject in which his position is unchallenged."

The Music Critic

Kodály' s short career as a music critic began in the autumn of 1917, amidst the deepening gloom and demoralization of the fourth year of war. Though he was to continue to write critical articles up to the 'fifties, many of them devoted to the work of his friend Bartók, his regular contributions to the literary journal, *Nyugat*, and later to the daily, *Pesti Napló*, came to an end in 1919, but in these two years he had shown himself to be, in Bartók's words, "the most clear-sighted critic in Hungary."

Typically enough, his first article was an appreciation of the Waldbauer-Kerpely Quartet, who, having made their professional *début* as interpreters of his music, had attracted considerable hostility from musical officialdom. And, later, it was after hearing them play the Sonata for Violoncello and Piano, that he wrote of Debussy: "Even in his most intentionally formless music... some Latin heritage saves him from formlessness. In a work such as this, despite its comparatively trivial content, many of his admirable qualities are displayed: perfect taste, an impeccable balance between form and content, terse precision, simplicity and euphony." Debussy's music had been the great experience of his first visit to Paris, and he was one of the first critics to write an enduring appreciation of it, in an obituary notice in April 1918. "His death at the age of 56 was, perhaps, premature, for despite the evidence of fatigue in some of his later works, his art was still developing. He was undoubtedly the most distinguished musician of his generation; and, in respect of his influence, the most productive... In his music he sought to portray, in pictures at once accurate and suggestive, the most transient moods, to express the unfolding of an emotion, to trace precisely the fluctuations of the spirit; and he achieved his aim. And in this there is something closely akin to impressionism in painting... For a long time to come, perhaps for ever, Debussy's music will remain a possession of the few. Yet, even to-day, his salutary influence is already universal. It may be that his legacy to us may prove to be the inspiration he has given, rather than what he actually achieved; that his educative influence will be more enduring than his music. For the compass by which he steered points to a purer, a more noble art... The journey upon which he embarked leads to Freedom and to Beauty. In this sense, it is irrelevant to assess how big an area of the new world he himself actually discovered. In extent it is not comparable with the domains carved out by the few truly great musicians. But within his own world he is a poet, and more than this no man can be."

As a critic, Kodály was much concerned with the work of the Budapest Opera, his articles always containing an appraisal of the composer as well as a critique of the performance. For example, when *Dinorah* was revived, he took the opportunity of giving a considered opinion of Meyerbeer's status as a composer. "Quite apart from the great success he had with the public, the superficial facts of his career may well have had a good deal to do with his having been erroneously regarded as one of the great masters," he wrote. "Meyerbeer may have been the last composer to pass through all the stages of development that were typical of the great international musicians of the past... In Italy, the Italian operas he wrote were a success... and this success was a necessary preliminary to his later French operas. Just as it is impossible to think of Haendel, Gluck or Mozart without remembering their Italian periods, so too one is aware that Bach and Haydn and Beethoven, though they travelled little outside their native countries, nevertheless stood at the meeting-place of several distinctive musical cultures. It is only since Wagner that the Germans have lost interest in any music but their own. And, more recently, this delusion that no musical culture existed outside Germany was widely accepted also in Hungary. But Meyerbeer was far from possessing the talent of the men in whose footsteps he was following, so that unlike them he was not capable of welding this diversity of foreign influences into a powerful and homogeneous whole. Exposed to such influences, these others grew in stature: Meyerbeer merely became an eclectic. You have only to consider him alongside Beethoven to discover two quite opposite types of artist, the *vates* and the *histrio*. The one, possessed by his daimon, grapples with the world in the effort to project his inspiration in its purest form, and must endure both unhappiness and lack of understanding. The other, with one eye constantly fixed on the public, is concerned primarily with the effect he can produce; and remains successful throughout his career."

After the first performance, in Budapest, of Strauss's *Ariadne* he commented bitterly: "Eagerly awaited for years, *Ariadne* is here at last. But its arrival has been too long delayed, for in the meantime Time has been moving at a faster pace than usual... Once Strauss was regarded as revolutionary; and not without reason, though his innovations were primarily of a technical order. But here we have only a great technician at play—a man who is no longer able to take anything seriously himself, and therefore has nothing to say to us."

Of a Beethoven concert in October 1918, at which Ernő Dohnányi was the soloist, he wrote: "Those who speak of a 'Beethoven cult,' or a 'Dohnányi cult,' are incapable of recognizing any spontaneous public interest as natural, unless it is directed to something completely worthless. But even if this *were* merely a cult, and not an indication that as last Beethoven is beginning to be generally known and appreciated in our country, it is precisely such cults that can help educate the public. No one who has listened to Dohnányi's playing over a number of years, even if it has only been because it was the fashion to do so, is likely to be taken in again by mere superficial brilliance and cheap emotion, the stock-in-trade of second-rate virtuosos... It would seem probable that such a supreme level of performance can only be attained by a player who is himself a creative artist, and who, as it were, improvises what is in itself ineluctable and imperative." And again writing of Dohnányi's playing, this time of Liszt's music, he said: "He succeeded in conveying to us as much of Franz Liszt's versatility as any musician could cram into a single evening. In the *Valse Impromptu* we admired the dandy of the *salons*, in *Venezia e Napoli*, the travelled man-of-the-world; we listened to the poet, seeking for intimacy in *Consolation*, and spinning mystic visions in *Legend*. He was most convincing, perhaps, in such works as the *Sonata in B minor*, which has for long been one of Dohnányi's most admired performances, works which, though full of French pathos, break new ground with their atmosphere of revolution. For Liszt's piano pieces, apart from their other qualities, offer a superb opportunity to the executant."

Of Ravel, whose *Piano Trio* was performed by the Waldbauer-Kerpely Quartet in January 1919, he wrote: "This interesting composer belongs to the new French school, but though Debussy is his starting-point, and though he shares many of his peculiarities of style, he is not to be regarded simply as an imitator. In Ravel, the incorporeal, ethereal music of Debussy is infused with an alien element, a savage determination which, though maybe it brings him closer to the world of everyday experience, prevents him from achieving so often the poetical quality of his master."

But stimulating and interesting as these critical views of Kodály undoubtedly are, especially when it is remembered that they were written forty years ago, it is in the long series of articles devoted to the work of his friend Bartók that his critical gift is most significantly displayed. The earliest of these is a critique of the *Second String Quartet*, which he wrote on the occasion of its first performance in March 1918. "If it is permissible in respect of mediocre talents to speak of development at all," he writes, "it will usually be found to be a development towards greater and more glittering complexity and artificiality. Such composers seek to deck out the little they have to say in ever more striking finery. By contrast, genuine talent, continually jettisoning whatever is not an organic part of itself, strives to dispense with superficial effects in order to attain a greater simplicity. This is the path that Bartók is clearly pursuing... In the hands of the epigoni, form has degenerated into more formalism, until we have reached the state of anarchy described as 'modernism'; in which category, despite the evidence, the impercipient seek to include Bartók. In fact, in his constructive understanding of form, Bartók is much more akin to the classical masters, and this essentially new departure is consistently displayed in the *String Quartet*. What emerges from the successive movements is not a series of different moods, but the continual evolution of a single, coherent, spiritual process. The impression conveyed by the work as a whole, though it is from the musical point of view formally perfect, is that of a spontaneous experience."

After hearing the first performance of *Prince Bluebeard's Castle*, he described Bartók's music as "a unique fusion of primitive simplicity with the most advanced contemporary culture. His music is completely homogeneous: a self-contained and unified structure, with scarcely a trace of borrowing or imitation... What is least accessible in it to the average musical intelligence are those elements of it that arise from its connexion with folk music." In particular, Kodály attached great importance to the fact that "by taking the road that leads to the freeing of our language, to the translation of its natural cadences into music, Bartók has done a great deal to advance the development of a genuinely Hungarian style of recitative. This is the first opera to be performed on an Hungarian stage in which the singing is throughout in a pure and undistorted Hungarian."

After the first performance of the *Rhapsody for Piano and Orchestra* in March 1919, Kodály noted that this work had had to wait fourteen years before it achieved a hearing, though in 1905 Bartók was already making a sweeping advance. "This work, which we can now see to have reached the highest level in the development of the Hungarian style up to that time, was the point of departure from which, ever since, he has been steadily ascending until he has attained his present commanding position." And almost a year later he reverted to the same theme, in an article he contributed to *Pesti Napló* on 22nd April, 1919—his last as a regular critic: "Nine years have elapsed since we last had the opportunity of hearing a whole evening's programme devoted to Bartók's music. The long succession of new works that he has written during these years have earned for him nothing but jeers and persecution, or the frivolous comment of causal 'music lovers' and obtuse and malicious newspaper critics. Yet Bartók has remained undaunted, sticking to his own road with the imperturbability of unerring instinct. Now, as one looks back, one recognizes in these works the faithful record of a gradual spiritual metamorphosis that has, as yet, only taken place in a few people. Yet the new spirit that is taking shape in these few is now just beginning to discover the kindred souls amongst the majority. This is not the time for splitting critical hairs about music that is bursting with vitality and explosive tension. But we can be certain that, when the day of reckoning comes, these works will be found amongst the few genuinely great ones that will be the basis for Hungary's claim to a place in the civilized world."

But though this was Kodály's last regular contribution, it was far from being his last tribute to his friend. In 1935, discussing a collection of Bartók's children's songs that had been published for Christmas, he wrote: "Children will readily understand them and experience an immediate sense of kinship, especially if, either by birth or education, they have already absorbed the atmosphere of folk music. They will understand them because Bartók addresses them without any of the pedantry of the teacher... he does not condescend to children, but treats them as fellow human-beings, in a way that only he is capable of doing, because in him, despite his white hair, the child has survived intact." And again, recalling him on the fifth anniversary of his death, he wrote: "In the course of the last fifty years there have been many attempts to write new music. All over the world a new spirit is emerging that is clamouring for artistic expression. Yet Bartók is one of the few who have had the ability to express this spirit in an enduring form, and for this reason he is one of the composers whose works are most frequently performed." Then, answering the question how we should best administer the legacy he has bequeathed to us, he went on: "Bartók's final and triumphant home-coming is dependent on our becoming a musically educated nation. And to achieve this aim demands co-operation from all sides. Once his music has reached those in whom it originated, the ordinary working people, once they have come to understand it, then we shall have true musical appreciation—then will the people of Hungary enjoy real happiness."

These words form a fitting conclusion to this survey of Kodály's work as a critic, for in them may be heard a voice that was to become increasingly characteristic of him, the voice of a man impelled by a growing sense of responsibility, who, ever since the nineteen-twenties, had been realizing with increasing clarity that the true critic must also be a teacher, prepared to undertake the arduous task of popularizing his subject. And this was a task that, as he himself put it in an address to the Academy of Sciences, "simply cannot be left to the dabblers and sciolists; a task that only the best of us are good enough to achieve."

THE TEACHER

Kodály's work as a teacher is like a theme and variations. Its central aim has been the creation of a national musical culture of European status, through the introduction of singing and solfeggio instruction on a nationwide basis and a great development of the choral movement. It recurs, sometimes openly, sometimes less explicitly, in almost all his writings and lectures; and many of his musical works were composed with a view to promoting the same aim. His work as a teacher, which began over fifty years ago in 1907 and still continues, shows an unbroken development. To begin with his main concern was the training of professional musicians; later, concerned with raising the whole level of musical life, he turned to the public, especially the youth, and set out to reform the system of musical instruction in the State schools; and finally he extended his work to the people as a whole. Thus, broadly speaking, his educational activities fall into three periods, which, though the last two overlap, may be considered separately.

Professor of Composition

When, in 1907, Kodály was appointed to fill the vacant Chair of Musical Theory at the Academy of Music, he was not yet twenty-five; and at the end of twelve months he took over the first-year students in the Faculty of Composition from the retiring Professor, Koessler. His appointment was a turning-point in the history of the Academy. From the time of Franz Liszt and Ferenc Erkel onwards a large proportion of the teaching staff had been Germans, amongst them such eminent scholars as Robert Volkmann, Hans Koessler and Viktor Herzfeld. Thanks to their efforts the Hungarian Academy quickly achieved a European reputation, but the language they taught in, and more significantly the whole spirit of their teaching, remained German. To change this state of affairs was the task of a new generation—a task that was achieved, not without difficulty, thanks to the efforts of such men as Ernő Dohnányi, Antal Molnár, Leó Weiner and, particularly, Bartók and Kodály.

Kodály soon came to the conclusion that the educational methods of the Academy were failing to provide a thorough musical training; and the remedy he proposed was a reform of the system of musical dictation and the introduction of solfeggio training. But as the Faculty proved to be unsympathetic and refused to support him, he was able to apply his methods only in his own classes. Two incidents that occurred at this time illustrate the official outlook of the Academy at this time. One hot summer's day, strolling through the town, he met the Director, Ödön Mihalovics, who took exception to the fact that he was carrying his overcoat over his arm instead of wearing it. "If it's not too hot for me to wear my overcoat properly," said the Director, "it won't kill you to do so. We can't have our Academy lecturers slouching about the streets like that." The second story Kodály has told himself: "I had given one of Dávid Popper's pupils, a fellow who hadn't been attending classes and had neglected his work throughout the year, a low mark for harmony. Popper, however, wanted me to mark him higher so that he could be admitted to the next class. 'He may as well carry on with his studies,' he said, 'he'll make a smart enough executant in time.' To which I replied: 'I had supposed, sir, that our job was to train all-round musicians, not merely players. It will hardly be of much credit to us if we turn out pupils without a thorough knowledge of music."

But if the official view was a combination of strict attention to purely formal questions with considerable laxity in respect of their musical training, Kodály's ambition was to produce thoroughly qualified musicians. With regard to the training of composers, the aim he set his students was, on the one hand to acquire the widest possible knowledge of musical literature, and on the other to work through, and discuss, the largest possible number of excercises. As to the efficacy of his method, the best proof of this is the fact that when he retired from the Academy the number of students making use of the musical archives dropped by half—a fact that, even in the official report, was attributed to the discontinuation of Kodály's classes. His own account of his educational principles is to be found in a speech he made at the time of the memorable attack on his work as a teacher:

"We have to assimilate all that is best in the musical heritage of Western Europe. I am doing my best to help my students to master the polyphonic style... Indeed, in this, I go further than anyone has ever done in this country, or even than is customary abroad. But our job is to turn out musicians who are not only European, but also Hungarian... It is only by a fusion of the traditions of both Europe and Hungary that we shall obtain results that are valid for Hungarians... Unless we are content for it to be confined to a small circle of people versed in foreign culture, the musical life of our country must be steeped in folk music... I am careful, especially at the start, not to overwhelm students of composition with folk music, since it is not my aim to provide a forcing-house for a national school of composers... One must always start by taking into account the inherent, individual disposition of one's students... And it is in this respect that I can claim to have made the fewest mistakes: of my thirteen students, no two of them could be confused, each of them is quite distinct from the others. But this respect for individual leanings must be applied equally—if we should not force our students into Hungarian uniform, neither should we insist on them wearing a German, or for that matter any other national, uniform."

We have quoted Kodály himself at some length, but also important are the views of his pupils. One of them, the late Mátyás Seiber, has said of his teaching: "With Kodály, instruction ceased to be merely instruction, and became something quite different. He has that curiously compulsive and suggestive power of drawing out from his pupils all their latent ability. It was not necessary for him to do much talking, and indeed he never said one word too many. But, precisely for this reason, everything he did say was all the more significant... One such word from Kodály was sometimes enough to change the whole direction of a man's life, suddenly illuminating a field of study that had till that moment been completely obscure... I don't believe there is another man living to-day, who teaches the rules of the old counterpoint so thoroughly, and so constructively, as he does... In the way he handles his students he is unique... In his own words, he allows them 'to grow from their own roots.' He makes no attempt to interfere in their development, but allows their personality to unfold in accordance with their individual bent. He does not recognize any pre-determined pattern... It would be a complete mistake, however, to suppose that Kodály therefore just leaves his pupils to shift for themselves... On the contrary, he has a clear plan of what he is doing and, without their suspecting it, he firmly leads them towards its fulfilment... And there is one thing no student of his could fail to learn from him: that talent alone is not enough to achieve one's goal, but must be backed by hard work and a thorough professional grounding." Another pupil, Zoltán Horusitzky, has written: "In his researches into the laws of style, he does not simply familiarize himself with the past, but relives it. And similarly, as a teacher of composition, he is at pains to initiate his students into the spirit of the masters: they have to write quartets in the style of Mozart, fugues in that of Bach, rondos of Couperin, and motets and masses in the style of Palestrina or of Orlando di Lasso."

Two other comments by former pupils are also worth quoting. Asked what he considered to be the secret of Kodály's great achievements as a teacher, Pál Kadosa[34] replied: "The high standards that he has always set for music, and indeed for all the arts; and the great discrimination he shows in every aspect of his teaching, demanding of his pupils that they should work and think absolutely independently." And Pál Járdányi[35], who studied under him in later years, has written: "He never talked about his own work, and indeed did not like us to refer to it. If he wanted to illustrate a point he would take an example from one of the masters, usually one of the greatest; and his extraordinary capacity for quoting music at will brought home to us the value of erudition. This, and his austerity—his well known 'ruthlessness'—were continual incentives to serious study... It was the combination of his fascinating power as an artist with his sober objectivity as a scholar that made his teaching quite unique."

In his teaching, as in his music, Kodály was always striving towards a higher synthesis: while urging his pupils to study the great music of Europe, he taught them at the same time to love and cherish the traditions of their own country. Whether he was lecturing or composing he was continually showing how the spirit of Hungary could be expressed in its own musical idiom, and how this idiom could at the same time be made a part of the great musical tradition of Europe. To-day there is scarcely a composer in the country who has not benefited from his guidance, for as Bartók once justly said: "Kodály is the greatest teacher of composition that Hungary has ever had."

Teacher of Youth

That Kodály's activities as a teacher were by no means confined to a limited circle of professional musicians is amply demonstrated by a few facts. Of his sixteen educational publications, six comprise several volumes, and each of these contain over a hundred musical exercises. Thirty-three of the articles he contributed to newspapers or magazines are devoted to the musical training of young people or the subject of children's choirs; while the number of choruses composed specially for children amount to nearly fifty. These figures alone are eloquent proof of his preoccupation with youth; and indeed, for several decades, one of his central aims as a teacher was to abolish musical illiteracy amongst children.

Looking back in 1937, Kodály recalled that: "Until 1925 I had lived the ordinary life of a professional musician. I was not concerned, that is to say, with our educational system because I assumed that it was satisfactory and that everything possible was being done; and that, as far as music was concerned, those who had no ear for it might just as well be written off. Then an incident occurred that destroyed this illusion. One fine spring day I happened to come across an outing of young girls in the hills of Buda. They were singing, and for half an hour I sat behind some bushes listening to them. And the longer I listened, the more appalled I was by the kind of songs they were singing..." His dismay increased when he discovered that they were students from a teachers' training college; and the fact that what they were singing was not merely trash, but actively harmful from an educational as well as a musical point of view, set him pondering as to what could be done about it. As a composer, the first idea that struck him was that it was up to him to provide them with alternative values, and he immediately put it into practice by writing *The Straw Guy* and *See, the Gypsy Munching Cheese*— the first in a long line of choral works. That his judgement of the situation had been correct was soon proved by the popular success the two choruses achieved and, subsequently, by the emergence of the Singing Youth movement[36]. But he realized that more than this was required if any serious impact was to be made on the type of music used in the schools with official support; and he therefore carried the battle into the press with a long series of articles and essays.

Gradually he succeeded in winning over a number of chorus leaders and teachers of singing, but if complete victory was to be achieved it still remained to effect a drastic reform of the methods of instruction in the schools. And for this it was necessary to provide suitable text-books—a task which, once again, fell upon him. His first study in this field, *Children's Choirs*, was published in 1929, by which time he had already gained considerable experience of the methods of teaching singing that were in use in the schools, as well as having composed about a dozen children's choruses. "What children are being taught to sing at school," he wrote, "is for the most part of no artistic value; and the way they are taught is worse than if they were left to themselves. After such a training they can hardly hope to experience music as an art for the rest of their lives. At best, they will pass on to the kind of choral society that is nothing more than an adult edition of school singing... This is the reason why, even amongst educated people, we so often find a disconcerting ignorance of music. A cultivated taste in literature and the fine arts is often accompanied by a childish ignorance of music, so that people who are prepared to fight for higher standards with their right hand actually encourage what is worthless with their left... Peasant children are in much closer contact with genuine art, for what they hear out of school belongs to the ancient and noble tradition of folk music... Bad taste is infectious. But while a deplorable fashion in dress may not be a very serious matter, since ugly clothes are not going to injure anyone's health, bad taste in the arts is as serious as a mental illness, for it has the effect of cauterizing susceptibility... Adults affected by this disease are for the most part in-

70

curable. What is needed is prophylaxis: it is in school that immunity from this contagion should be provided... But to-day, far from doing this, our schools are actually helping to spread the disease... Singing, music, ought to be taught in such a way that children acquire a lasting appetite for the best music. It is no good approaching this problem in an abstract, rational way... We must encourage intuition and spontaneity. Often, a single musical experience in childhood is enough to awaken a lifelong appreciation. But the provision of such experience must not be left to chance—it is a matter for the school."

And he continued, more severely: "We have got to get rid of the pedagogic superstition that some sort of diluted substitute for art is good enough as the material for teaching. No one is more instinctively susceptible to pure art than the child, for as young people recognize in their hearts, in every great artist there is a survival of the child. Indeed, the superstition should be completely reversed: only the best art is good enough for children, anything else will only do them harm." And turning to the composers, he added: "If only Erkel had written one or two short choral works for children, his operas would now appeal to a far greater number of people. Nobody should be above writing for children: on the contrary, we should strive to become good enough to do so. What is needed is original music, works that by their words, melody and atmosphere are adapted to the voice and spirit of children."

If, in Hungary in the nineteen-thirties, the appreciation of music was still somewhat superficial, the reason is to be found in the misconceived cultural policy of the preceding decades, which was primarily concerned with the musical education of the upper strata of society. The Budapest Academy of Music trained excellent musicians—for other countries. At home there were no audiences to appreciate them, because no one had been concerned with the musical training of the masses of the people. As Kodály pointed out in 1945: "For the great bulk of ordinary people, school has been a deterrent to the enjoyment of art, and in later life nothing has been done to encourage such enjoyment." And yet, as he declared on another occasion: "Until the broad masses of the people enjoy the benefits of music, we cannot speak of a genuine national culture." He developed this idea further in an article on "Musical Life in a Provincial Town": "Education of an élite and education of the masses must go hand-in-hand: only if we maintain equilibrium between the two shall we obtain results of permanent value. The most urgent step towards restoring such equilibrium is the development—or, more accurately, the creation—of musical training in the schools." To this end it was necessary to have, in contrast with the past, "a sufficiency of teachers, of material and of time."

71

But though Kodály was able to diagnose the causes of the lack of musical appreciation in his country, and to suggest the correct remedy, until 1945 there was but little improvement in the situation, because before that his view received no official support. Nevertheless, even without such support, he carried on with his prodigious efforts to effect a change. Later, looking back on those years, he said: "Obviously, something had to be done to try to create a demand for more and better music. In my search for what could be done, I was drawn towards the younger—and still younger—people, until at last I arrived at the nursery school. But though my article on "Music for the Nursery School" was received with intense displeasure, it was necessary to point out what was the root of the evil, because the older people grow the more difficult they are to cure."

This article, which spared neither official feelings nor individual interests, led to considerable controversy when it was first published in 1941. In the preface Kodály insisted: "The real trouble with our culture is that it has been built from the top downwards. When the restrictions which for centuries have cramped our national life were lifted, we were in too much of a hurry to make up for lost opportunities... Culture is a plant of slow growth: you can neither accelerate its pace nor alter the order of its evolution. We began by carving the ornamental pinnacles, and only thought about building the walls when it became clear that the whole edifice was tottering. Even now the foundations have not been properly laid—and this is especially so with regard to musical appreciation." In this respect he pointed to the failure of the teaching of singing in the schools; and drew attention to the responsibility of professional musicians for this failure: "(their) negligence is undoubtedly one of the reasons why our schools have become the musical wilderness they are."

From this he went on to urge that systematic training in the appreciation of music ought to start at a still earlier age, in the nursery school, "for it is there, while at play, that children will learn what it will be too late to teach them when they get to primary school... Modern psychology assures us that, in the education of the child, the period from three to seven years old is of greater importance than the succeeding years. Anything that is left out, or badly taught, during those years cannot be remedied later on. The future development of a human being, perhaps his whole life, is decided in those years... If the spiritual life remains more or less uncultivated for the first seven years it will not bring to fruition the seeds that are planted in it later." Then he turned to an examination of the printed material available for teaching singing in nursery schools, and summarized its defects under four heads: "1. It excludes our national heritage, so that it fails to lay the foundations on which to build later a Hungarian musical consciousness. 2. By the inclusion of foreign elements it hinders the development of spontaneous musical taste and encourages an alien appreciation of music. 3. The poor quality of so many of the tunes can only draw the children's attention to trash, instead of towards good music. 4. It fails entirely to develop the child's grasp of music to the fullest extent possible."

Recently, when this article was republished in 1957, Kodály added an epilogue, summarizing the advances achieved since 1947 and criticizing the defects that still remained. In particular, he expressed his disapproval of the constant use of the piano in the teaching of songs and choral music, for the following reasons: "(a) It robs the child of the pleasure, and the benefit, to be derived from unaccompanied singing. If you always use crutches, you will end by being unable to walk without them. (b) The piano does not correspond to the inevitable fall in pitch of the child's voice. I have heard children's choral works where the choir has dropped two or three tones in pitch while the accompanying piano remained where it was. (c) Even if it is tuned daily, the tempered piano is always out of tune, and therefore cannot teach pure singing. (d) Though they may have to be sung indoors, children songs should always convey an illusion of the open air, which the piano makes impossible. (e) Continual piano accompaniment to the telling of a fairy-tale is superfluous, and becomes a caricature of programme music. The child who becomes accustomed to the portrayal of processes external to the music will never understand music... If the singing is invariably accompanied on the piano, the child will never learn to appreciate pure, virginal, melody— yet this is what it should learn first of all." And he concludes by urging his "young colleagues who write symphonies" to take every opportunity "of dropping in at a nursery school now and then. For that is where it is being decided whether or not there will be an audience to appreciate your music in twenty years' time."

But Kodály's interest in musical education was by no means confined to the nursery school. Important as he considered this to be, since it was here that a solid foundation could be laid, he was equally concerned with the teaching in the secondary schools. Prior to 1945, even in those schools where music was included in the syllabus, the shortage of qualified teachers was such that only a few of the pupils acquired any proficiency in reading music. When, therefore, around 1940, the students' musical society movement began to gather momentum, Kodály did everything he could to encourage it and, in 1944, he wrote an article, "The Purpose of School Musical Societies," expressing his views on the subject. Their function, he considered, was not to promote the composing of music—"that will always be the business of the elect"—but to develop sound musical taste and abolish musical illiteracy. "The way to the enjoyment of good music," he wrote, "is open to all... By taking part in choral singing everyone may gain intimate experience of great geniuses and make of them lifelong companions. Boys who show special aptitude may take up the instrument that appeals to them... but singing, which is accessible to all, should be the main concern of the Society. In addition to the school choir, groups of three or four singers should be formed, who should begin by practising singing simple exercises in unison and then proceed to more difficult ones, with different styles of melody. The responsibility of singing an independent part is the best way of acquiring a general musical understanding."

Following the Liberation of Hungary in 1945 there was some improvement in the teaching of music: a new syllabus was drawn up and became part of the general syllabus for secondary schools; and the principle of teaching by professionals was accepted. Nevertheless, progress was slow, and Kodály did his best to speed it up. Realizing that the pupils at the secondary schools were in need of help, he took up the cudgels on their behalf when, in 1953, the *Magyar Nemzet* opened its columns to a debate on the teaching of drawing and music: "The people have every right to expect," he wrote, "that the State schools, which are run on their money, should lead their children to a full development of their human capacities by training their mental powers and physical skills. Can we speak of a fully developed human being who is incapable of appreciating the arts? Of course not. He would be but the rump of a man, and his life would be a bleak one... Music teaches us to hear, and drawing to see, things... and what could be better than choral singing for developing a sense of community? Solo performances tend to generate selfishness and vanity, but, for the members of a choir, the knowledge that even the seemingly unimportant ones play an important part, the feeling that each is but a drop in the sea and that, though the choir could get on without him, a single slip on his part would ruin the total effect—such feelings underline the need for individual responsibility within a communal effort. And what could provide a better training for Socialism?... Our system of training professional musicians has got its own problems, but as yet we haven't even begun to tackle the problem of providing musical education for the public. To do that we must begin in the primary school, and nowhere else. Our aim must be to turn out children for whom music, good music, is a necessity of life..."

We have seen how Kodály's concern for the development of musical education found expression, first in the series of works for children's choirs, beginning in 1925, and later in the press campaign he carried on from 1929 onwards. But in 1937 he embarked on yet another side of his educational activity, the provision of music manuals, suitable for use in schools. The first of these, the four-volume *Bicinia Hungarica*, was immediately welcomed by the critics, who hailed it as "an introduction to music-reading and two-part singing, as well as to the treasure-house of Hungarian music, not by means of abstract exercises, but in the living spirit of children's play-songs and folk songs." Though neither this nor the several similar collections that followed it became compulsory reading in the schools (this status was accorded for the first time to the *Songs for Schools*, published in 1943), it was widely used by music teachers who appreciated its educational value. In the Foreword Kodály recalls his barefooted companions at the Galánta primary school. "It was of you I was thinking while I was writing this book," he says. "If only we had been taught such things, and many others, what a different kind of life we might have created for our country. That remains a task for those who are now beginning to learn that it isn't worth much just to sing for one's self: it is so much better when two people sing together. And the number will grow, until there are hundreds upon thousands, all intoning the great harmony which unites us. Then only shall we be able to say truthfully 'Let the whole world rejoice'!" And in the Epilogue, commenting on the harmful influence of tunes and methods imported from Germany, in answer to his own question as to whether foreign songs ought to be sung, he replies emphatically: "Of course they should. But not in the way we have tended to sing them up to now—camouflaged as Hungarian songs. We must state clearly where they come from... Are we to go on getting everything second-hand? Altered to suit the tastes of a nation which, in thought and feeling, differs from us more widely than any other nation of Western Europe? Germany only intercepts our view of the West... By all means let us draw upon original sources. But, while learning whatever may be of benefit to us from every nation, let us make sure that we become the intellectual colony of none."

In this collection about one in four of the songs is a folk song for which Kodály has written an accompanying voice, the others he composed himself; but the difference in style between the two groups is almost imperceptible. There are, in addition, twenty-four songs without words, that are designed to introduce the child to the secrets of solmization. Taken as a whole, the one hundred and eighty exercises contained in these four volumes not only display Kodály's brilliant gift for counterpoint, but they also almost completely free the pupil from the limitations of vertical thinking and instrument-playing. Moreover, by creating a system of pentatonic counterpoint they provide the technical basis for the building up of a national music; while at the same time these little pieces, by the variety of their style and rhythm, are a source of delight as well as of instruction.

In addition to Hungarian songs, Kodály also included in this collection a number of songs belonging to kindred peoples, especially the two-part adaptations of fifty-seven Mari and three Finnish folk songs in volume four. His reason for doing so is explained in the Epilogue: "Magna Hungaria was swept away by the Tartar invasion, but it did not disappear without trace. There are still songs that do not sound very different whether they are sung on the banks of the Danube or the banks of the Volga... For us, the lesson of this is that, so long as we do not forget who we are, we shall survive... No matter how profound a knowledge we have of Hungarian music, our understanding of it will only have perspective and depth to the extent that we also take into account the music of peoples that are akin to us... Even when they differ most widely from ours, their songs are still of more help to us in broadening our general musical knowledge than the songs of Western Europe would be."

From 1937 onwards, Kodály has continued to publish a whole number of similar collections, having the same purpose in view. Next in order to the *Bicinia* was *Let us Sing Correctly*, published in 1941 and consisting of a hundred and seven choral exercises for two voices. In these tunes without words, rhythmical difficulties, and the use of semi-tones, are avoided, since their primary purpose is to teach clear intonation, a question that had hitherto received but little attention. Most teachers and choir leaders had assumed that singing was true if it was in tune with the piano, but as Kodály points out in the Preface, "the purity of choral singing depends on maintaining acoustically clear intervals, which are distinct from the tuning of a piano." He therefore holds that the beginner should be accompanied, not by the piano, but by a second voice; and that this is equally important for training the ear for polyphony and for ensuring the purity of solo singing. For, "if you only sing solo songs you will never learn to sing true. It is only through part-singing that one can master true solo singing." The clear intonation affects the fullness and beauty of the sound of the chorus as well.

It was with the same aim in mind that he later published *Two-Voice Singing Exercises* and *Tricinia*, though these were also intended to make the supposed difficulties of polyphonic music intelligible to wider circles of people. And in this connection mention should also be made of the nine *Epigrams* (1954), originally described as "a one-voice reading exercise"; though on account of their exceptional beauty and of the fact that, later, very beautiful words were specially written for them, these are discussed later, amongst the songs.

76

So far, the manuals we have discussed were designed primarily to introduce children to polyphonic music. But Kodály also produced manuals in support of his conviction that the creation of a truly Hungarian musical culture could only result from the interaction between European art music and the folk music of Hungary. Such were the *333 Reading Exercises*, the four-volume *Pentatonic Music* and the *24 Little Canons on the Black Keys*. The first of these was a pioneer work. In it the compass of the songs, for the most part restricted to six notes, is within the capacity of the youngest children. But because of "the widespread practice of only practising the singing of intervals in ascending leaps," they contain numerous examples of descending leaps, since the singing of such intervals "involves an entirely different mental process, and is more difficult." Of the content of this collection Kodály noted: "If we want the light of our ancient folk song to be diffused throughout the whole people, as once it was, we must prepare our children for it by giving them short easy tunes, written in the style and spirit of the originals. If we fail to do this, and they are brought up on the musical material used in our schools to-day they are bound to regard... our most ancient national music... as some kind of oddity. It is a complete mistake to start with the diatonic scale, and then, later on, to study the pentatonic scale as a strange historical phenomenon."

In *Pentatonic Music*, which represents a further stage on the same road, the tunes are recorded, without the use of notes and lined paper, simply by solmization. Yet this revival of an old method of transcription is not essential to the purpose of the collection, but is simply used as a means of developing the ear without the visual aid of a score. The primary purpose of these four hundred and forty songs is to popularize the pentatonic scale, and the importance of this is underlined by Kodály in a note to the second volume: "1. It is easier to sing true without semitones; 2. Musical understanding and the ability to sing true are developed more effectively when the extent of the intervals varies (pentatony), than when it is always the same (as in the case of the diatonic scale); and 3. Only in this way can we instil in our children a genuinely Hungarian musical consciousness." As in the whole corpus of Hungarian folk song the proportion of short songs is comparatively small, Kodály had here to draw partly on his own resources, partly on the songs of kindred peoples—the hundred short marching songs in the second volume were all written by him in the years 1941-42, in an attempt to provide teachers with an alternative to the hideous songs then in use in the schools. The third and fourth volumes contain a hundred Mari and a hundred and forty Chuvash tunes respectively, the reason for which is explained in a note to the last volume: "Anyone who has once mastered the difficult rhythms of Chuvash, Mari and other oriental songs will find the complicated rhythms of modern music much easier to deal with. As the world is more and more opened up, art that is confined to a single people will sooner or later become meaningless. A universal music is nearer to realization to-day than is Goethe's conception of a universal literature. The question that faces us is, whether we can best hold our own in world music by sacrificing our individual characteristics or by emphasizing them? Some think that it is by the former method that we shall become the best citizens of the musical world. My own view, on the contrary, is that the more intensively we study and cultivate our own music, the more we shall be able to contribute to world music."

In the *24 Little Canons on the Black Keys* Kodály was breaking new ground in the teaching of the piano. They spring from the idea that, as in the case of singing, instrumental studies should start with pentatonic melodies. By beginning with exercises on the black keys "the pentatonic scale can be seen as a distinct, self-contained system: it doesn't have to be extracted from the heptatonic like some kind of gap-toothed monstrosity... It is much more profitable to begin with the black keys than to keep on hammering away at the white. And, intellectually, the advantages are inestimable." The first sixteen pieces are transcribed in solmization signs, and only the last eight are scored conventionally. By beginning his studies in this way the student "will first obtain an understanding of the meaning of the notes, and only then proceed to learn the symbols for them." Two other points of interest here are, firstly, that the two parts are recorded on the same line; and, secondly, that the eight conventionally scored canons are intended to be played a semitone higher than the score indicates. The purpose of this is to develop musical thinking and a facility for transposition. The principles embodied in this, and in the previously discussed works, have to-day become the basis both for musical training and for the teaching of singing in schools, the two aspects of musical education which Kodály has always regarded as being inseparable.

Though Kodály did not neglect the training of professional musicians during these years, he continued to devote his attention primarily to the schools, which he considered to be the main front in the struggle for a national musical culture. An important contribution to this was the *Songs for Schools*, a collection containing 630 songs for use in the eight forms of the primary school, though of great value also for teaching in nursery and secondary schools. Designed as an introduction to the study of "the musical mother tongue," it is a selection of folk songs, Hungarian historical songs, nineteenth century art songs and folk songs from the neighbouring countries. Together with Jenő Ádám's *Manual of Singing* it became, for a time, compulsory in schools, and though it was withdrawn in 1948 it strongly influenced the text-books adopted in its place. Another of Kodály's projects that was realized as the result of the Liberation was the "preparatory music course," which, on his initiative, was opened at Pécs in 1945, and which was to lead to the institution of the first "musical primary school" at Kecskemét five years later. The success of these experiments may be judged by the fact that in the following decade more than a hundred such schools were opened all over the country.

There remains yet another aspect of Kodály's educational work, the one which has so far attained the least success, and which for that reason, perhaps, occupies the centre of his interest—the introduction of solfeggio instruction and solmization with the movable Doh. As early as 1907, inspired by the success of this method in France and Italy, Kodály had realized its importance, but until 1945 all his efforts to introduce it in Hungary met with stubborn official resistance. To-day, however, thanks to his help and guidance, teachers have available as a basis for teaching solfeggio Erzsébet Szőnyi's excellent text-book, *The Methods of Reading and Writing Music,* published in 1954-56, and supplemented by eight volumes of exercises.

In his Preface to this book will be found Kodály's views on the subject. "That the teaching of music is best begun with singing," he writes, "that it is through singing, and before ever touching an instrument, that the child should learn to read music, are recognized as truths by a good many people. But though in this country they have found advocates, they are by no means generally accepted here, even to-day." And the reason for this failure in his opinion is that "while in the world around us the transition from a culture founded on oral tradition to a culture based on a written tradition has long since taken place, in Hungary, though we have effected this transition in literature, in music we still have one foot in a purely oral culture. Thus, unless we want to be left behind for good, there is no more urgent task confronting us than to make this transition in music also." And, criticizing the inadequacy of earlier music teaching, he continues: "Mechanical training in instrumental playing, without corresponding theoretical education; music-making with the fingers instead of with the soul; the omission of any thorough musical grounding; and neglect of solfeggio—these are the direct causes of the present decadence of singing and of the increasing number of second-rate professional musicians and amateurs who over-rate their own capabilities... A variety of obstacles have, up to now, prevented the setting up of a really systematic method of solfeggio teaching—let alone its use on a national scale... But the study of solfeggio must be continued unceasingly up to the highest level of musical education, both vocal and instrumental, until music can be read, as books are by educated adults, silently, but with a full mental comprehension of the sounds"—or, as he once put it in a telling aphorism: "Anyone who calls himself a musician, must be able to hear what he sees and see what he hears... If we want to set professional musical training on a proper footing in this country we must pick up the thread at the point where Liszt dropped it. Fortunate is the child who expresses the first ideas it associates with a musical score by means of its own voice, for once it has been accustomed to sing only with the technique of an instrument in mind, it becomes extremely difficult for it to grasp that singing is primary. And, indeed, if it never sings with its own voice, it will only achieve real, uninhibited, intimate singing on any other instrument with the greatest difficulty, if at all. Not even the greatest talent can ever fully overcome the drawbacks that result from a musical training that has not been based on singing."

The principles here enunciated by Kodály are admirably exemplified in Szőnyi's book, to which they form the Introduction. The hundred lessons it comprises are so arranged that it can be used with advantage not only in professional training at all levels, but also in schools and in work with choirs. The aim of solfeggio is to equip the pupil with such a mastery of music that he is able to transpose the visual image of the score almost automatically into sound that he can sing; and, at the same time, to transcribe on paper the sounds that he hears. In short, it aims to establish a living unity between the aural and the visual aspects of music. As it is practised in Hungary, under the influence of Kodály, the pupils are drawn into collective music-making, using the simplest of all musical instruments: their own voices. In this way those who are studying an instrument acquire a real understanding of music independent of the instrument, and a proficiency which, without solfeggio, would inevitably be mechanical.

At a more advanced stage of the curriculum the students begin to learn solmization, with the movable Doh, the basis of which is that the keynote of every major scale, whatever its position may be in staff notation, is Doh. Thus solmization goes beyond the mere reading of music, and is able to express the character and tonality of the various keys. It therefore has a double significance: on the one hand it teaches the pupil to sing from the score, without having first had to learn to recognize all the notes in the staff notation; and on the other, it trains him to recognize immediately the tonality of the keys and to understand the specific qualities and harmonic structure of the melodies he is singing. The effect of the movable Doh is to develop a sense of the functional character of the notes of the scale, together

Kodály, with his Wife Emma, and Bartók (Taken during a tour
in Transylvania, 1912)

Kodály at the Outbreak of the First World War

with the ability to recognize musical intervals. Thus its practical value, both at elementary and advanced levels of study, is considerable. The conservative argument against its use, that it prevents the student from getting to know the conventional staff notation, is false. In fact, far from preventing such knowledge it lays the foundation for it, for the student who begins with the movable Doh system, and goes on to reading music in the fixed Doh system, is able to reach the stage of learning staff notation in his first year.

The fact is that the solfeggio system should not be regarded either as complete in itself or as universally valid, for, like music itself, it is being continually developed. Moreover the system itself is not the only factor that has to be considered: allowances also have to be made for national characteristics, as well as for the educational and cultural level of the pupils. Nevertheless there is reason to believe that the modern system of solfeggio, evolved by Kodály from the French and Italian systems, has an educational value for other countries besides Hungary. Though his primary concern has perhaps been to awaken a national musical consciousness in his fellow countrymen, Kodály's work as a teacher, by virtue of his exceptional erudition, acquires universal significance. The war on musical illiteracy, the struggle to raise the whole level of musical education, constitute one of the brightest pages in the history of Hungarian culture in the twentieth century. And that struggle, which thanks to the vigorous support of the socialist State is already beginning to succeed, will always be inseparably associated with the name of Kodály.

Music Belongs to Everybody

Kodály's conception of musical education has not been limited to the training of either professionals or young people. He realized that if it was to result in a genuine renascence of music it must in some measure involve the whole people; and, moreover, that it must have its roots in the still living heritage of Hungarian folk music. In this wider educational sphere his period of maximum activity was not to begin until about 1940, but as early as 1906, in the preface to *Hungarian Folk Songs*, he had stated his position. "It will be a long time," he wrote, "before these pristine manifestations of the spirit of our people come to occupy their rightful place in either our private or our public musical life. The overwhelming majority of us are not nearly Hungarian enough—neither sufficiently unsophisticated nor sufficiently well-educated—for these songs to find their way straight to our hearts. 'Hungarian folk songs in our concert halls'—how strangely that still sounds to-day. But the time will come when our folk music will be heard with the masterpieces of world music and with the folk songs of other nations. It will come when we begin to have concerts of Hungarian music in our own homes, and when music-loving families are no longer content with imported music-hall songs of the poorest quality or the products of our domestic pseudo-folk-song factories. It will come when, once again, we have Hungarian singers."

That in this first criticism of the Hungarian people for their lack of musical taste Kodály should also have spoken in defence of Hungarian folk song was no mere coincidence, for the determination to win recognition for the popular musical heritage, and to revive it before it finally became extinct, is central to his whole activity. In the programme for his first concert of folk songs in 1925 he said: "Is it not a symptom of a most serious illness that the finest songs that have been produced by the musical genius of Hungary in a thousand years are to-day remembered only by farm-hands and old peasants? Is it not our urgent duty to learn these songs from them, so that once again they may become the property of the whole people? Already in the villages the tradition is dying, and if the young folk are not going to carry it on it is up to us to do so, for the flame must never be allowed to go out." And again and again, in articles, lectures and speeches, he was to return to the attack, proclaiming the merits of the native folk music and berating his countrymen for their neglect of it.

In view of this, the question may arise, why was such persistence necessary on Kodály's part, since it is surely in the natural order of things that the art music of any nation develops naturally out of its folk music? This is what had happened in Britain, France, Germany, Italy, Russia and Spain, and though in most cases the process had been completed centuries earlier, it was not uncommon for composers to turn back to this treasure-house in search of fresh inspiration. But in this respect the case of Hungary was an exception, partly because the evolution of art music occurred much later there than in the rest of Europe, and partly because, by the time this evolution became possible, the vital spirit of folk music was in danger of being lost. To understand the reasons for this, it is necessary to recall one or two historical facts.

In the fourteenth and fifteenth centuries Hungary was still one of the leading countries in Europe, but in 1526 she lost that position at the disastrous battle of Mohács (see Note 5), as a result of which the greater part of the country came under the rule of the Ottoman Empire, while the remainder was split up between the Austrian emperors and the Magyar princes. Nearly two centuries were to pass before the Turks were finally expelled; and even then, for another hundred and fifty years and despite successive wars of independence, the Hungarian people were to remain under the dominion of the Austrian Habsburgs, who treated the 'liberated' country as conquered territory. Though they were Kings of Hungary, the Habsburgs were first and foremost Emperors of Austria, and they had no interest in assisting devastated Hungary to recover her economic strength or to make progress in the arts and sciences. Since the royal court was in Vienna, not in Budapest, it was there that the aristocracy spent the greater part of the year, and as a result the intellectual and artistic life of the country tended to be centred there as well, so that the gradual cultural revival in Hungary was largely dominated by the German spirit.

So powerful was this influence that, by the time Bartók and Kodály appeared on the scene, it had almost proved fatal to Hungarian music. The academic composers and artists were German-trained, while those who comprised the romantic Magyar movement were for the most part amateurs, who, insofar as they made use of native folk material at all, distorted it by the alien and uncongenial forms in which they clothed it. Amongst the people this division went even further: on the one hand, the educated minority would have nothing at all to do with Hungarian music; on the other, the great majority regarded all developed art music as something essentially foreign. For this state of affairs the gypsy orchestras were in large measure responsible, for, as Kodály noted, "as a result of their splendid imitative faculty they have acquired a genuinely Hungarian style of playing, but, as so often happens, the imitation tends to drive out the original. To-day, there is still a minority of our people who accept as genuinely Hungarian only such music as is played by the gypsies."

In the light of the above it is perhaps easier to understand Kodály's insistence that at the centre of the problem was the necessity of "making the musically educated more Hungarian, and the Hungarian people more musically educated." As he wrote in 1935 in an article called "Popular Tradition and Musical Culture": "Folk music is not primitive music, but an art that has matured in an evolutionary process lasting a thousand years... So far, it is the most consummate musical expression of our national spirit. Folk music has not fulfilled its function simply by providing a musical culture for the peasantry: it still has vital significance for all of us. For it contains the germ of a genuinely national musical culture, which it is the responsibility of the educated sections of our people to develop and bring to fruition. They will only find the strength to do this, however, to the extent that they achieve spiritual unity with the peasantry. It cannot be too often repeated that, if we are to become a nation, we must first of all become a people...

To this end, in addition to the work of individual composers, we need a complete renascence of our whole musical life. The towns must throw open their gates to welcome the ancient traditions that have been exiled to the villages, and, at the same time. the opportunity for elementary musical training must be provided in the countryside. If the villages inspire the towns with the true spirit of Hungary, and if the towns introduce genuine culture into the villages, then we may hope to see the emergence of a truly national culture."

In articles written in 1945 he expressed himself more strongly: "For the last seventy years musical education in this country has been on the wrong lines, and has therefore been utterly fruitless. We have been trying to teach people to appreciate music by ignoring and brushing aside precisely the music with which they were familiar, despite the fact that, if you want to build, you must use the foundations that are available—in our case, the heritage of folklore." And in another article, written in the same year, "The Next Step," he wrote: "The people of Hungary as a whole are at home with homophonic music. In it they have written masterpieces, and they have performed it with distinction. The next step is to initiate them into the secrets of polyphonic music, and to guide them towards the great music of the world... We have to discover the polyphonic style that emerges naturally from the laws governing Hungarian melody... To advance from music in one dimension to music in many dimensions is the democratic way forward."

In the early nineteen-fifties Kodály was once again provoked into controversy by the widely expressed opinion that "we must get beyond folk song." "This is quite true," he retorted. "We must, indeed. But before we can begin to do so, we must first get as far as folk song. If our people are to achieve the status of a nation, their music must first become the property of the nation. To reach this position is in the interest not only of the further development of our music, but also of our general musical and scientific culture." In connection with the proposed edition of the *Thesaurus of Hungarian Folk Music* he remarked: "This collection will have a lasting practical influence, and not only on our national life. After much dispute and misunderstanding, it is now clear to everyone that it is only by following this road that we shall achieve our own national style. We shall seek it elsewhere in vain." And his latest expression of the same belief was in 1957: "Folk song is one of the mighty corner-stones on which our nation can be rebuilt. The songs of the people are the heralds of life—of life that goes on for ever."

Side by side with his campaign for a proper appreciation of the importance of folk song Kodály carried on a persistent struggle to improve the scope and quality of choral singing. In 1941 he declared: "A musical culture that has real depth must always be founded on singing... The playing of instruments is inevitably a matter for the privileged few. Only the human voice, the most freely accessible and yet the most beautiful of all instruments, can provide the basis for a musical culture embracing the great majority." And if really large masses of people were to be brought into contact with great music, this meant that singing must be carried on by mixed choirs.

To begin with, this idea did not find easy acceptance. In Hungary the choral movement is of comparatively recent origin, dating back only to the eighteen-seventies, and, therefore, strongly under the predominant German influence. Moreover, it was not the spirit of the "Chorverein" that prevailed, but of the much shallower "Liedertafel," which, as Kodály noted in an article on "Hungarian Choral Singing": "had smuggled in the spirit of the German philistine, transforming Hungarians into petty-bourgeois Germans before our own urban civilization had had a chance to develop from its own roots." Under this influence, the male voice choirs that survived—often for reasons that had little to do with art—were from the artistic point of view useless, and even harmful.

Accordingly, from the nineteen-thirties onwards Kodály set about reforming them. On the one hand he sought to provide them with a new repertory by composing suitable music, such as the *Songs of Karád* and *The Bachelor*; and, on the other, he urged them to transform themselves into mixed voice choirs. Yet progress was slow, and, in 1942, we find him returning to the attack in an article entitled "Towards New Goals." Having set out the main objectives—the creation of mixed voice choirs and the introduction of training in music reading and solmization—he went on to blame the members of the choirs "for allowing themselves to be treated like parrots, and not insisting on being taught to read scores... Many choirs spend the entire year practising their prize entry for the singing competition, whereas, if only they had learned to read music, they would have been able not only to have broadened their own intellectual horizon, but also to have delighted their audiences with ten or twenty new choruses... One of the most harmful results of continually singing with a piano accompaniment is that people sing off-key. A whole number of our choral societies constantly sing out of tune, without the slightest realization of the fact." He also blamed the conductors for not recognizing the value of training in solmization as an aid, not only to the reading of scores, but also to clear intonation. And he concluded by stressing the need for well-trained conductors and carefully selected programmes. "Technical perfection," he said, "is dependent upon a sound moral outlook... And there is such a thing as amoral virtuosity. A perfect rendering of a shoddy work is like filling a golden cup from a puddle: the drink is in no way improved, and the soul remains empty."

In his efforts to raise the general level of musical culture, Kodály turned his attention first to the villages. Later, however, he extended his activities to the working class, realizing that they, like the peasantry, constitute "that homogeneous mass of people, thinking and feeling in the same kind of way, without which it is impossible for choral singing to flourish." He urged his own pupils to give assistance to workers' choirs. This idea would not even have occurred earlier to a musician who had graduated from the Academy of Music. But here he came up against a fresh obstacle: the refusal of the workers' choirs to sing folk songs. Eventually, however, he was able to convince them that, by so doing, "far from lowering themselves to the cultural level of the peasantry, they would be participating in a broader and richer, a more universal, human community."

There remains one further field, this time not directly connected with music, in which Kodály has influenced Hungarian culture. This is the pronunciation of colloquial Hungarian, which, in the nineteen-thirites, showed a marked deterioration. At the University Kodály had studied philology, and it was one of his masters at college, Zoltán Gombocz,[37] who drew his attention to Sievers's studies in the melody of language and encouraged him to undertake similar research. In 1937, in a lecture to the Eötvös College Society, Kodály noted that "setting poems to music, and trying to bring out the melodies that are latent in them, is in a sense a kind of experimental phonetics." The deterioration in spoken Hungarian he explained by historical causes: "In countries that have developed normally," he said, "the educated classes have exercised a decisive influence upon colloquial usage... In our country, as a result of our historical development, the most distinguished social circles have consistently shirked their responsibilities with regard to the fostering of national culture. It is impossible to accept either their habits of speech or their pronunciation as a model... In correct speech there are certain elements which, though audible, cannot be recorded in writing; and it is these elements that are especially prone to corruption."

This corruption he attributed to the fact that alien peoples had been absorbed into the Hungarian nation, as well as to the lack of any consistent speech training, the increasing use of foreign languages, and the number of operas and operettas that were translated from foreign languages. "To preserve the purity of spoken Hungarian," he insisted, "is as vitally important as to maintain our sentence structure and our stock of words." And he concluded by proposing the publication of a Hungarian phonetic dictionary and the institution of competitions in pronunciation for students.

The following year he carried the campaign further, in a lecture on the wireless: "It seems to be assumed," he said, "that as Hungarian is spoken by everybody, it does not matter whether our pronunciation is good or bad, so long as we can make ourselves understood. Certainly no attempt is being made to improve it." And after analyzing the causes leading to the corruption of speech, he went on: "Once you have made up your mind to achieve a correct pronunciation, it is only a question of time and diligence. It is true that those who have not acquired it by inheritance will have to work hard to master it; nor is it to be retained without considerable care. Moreover, for those who decide to do so, one thing is necessary: that they shall love Hungarian above any other language... The first thing to get right is the psychological basis of speech and pronunciation. Once we have done that, improvement will follow automatically."

In 1939 the first public Competition for Correct Pronunciation was organized, under the auspices of the Faculty of Philology of Budapest University, in which thirty-seven competitors took part. The winners were awarded prizes, and their speeches were broadcast on the national network; and for several years the Competition was repeated. At the 1941 Competition Kodály warned university students that "something more is at issue than the mere question of speech. Speech, pronunciation, is only an expression of, is dependent on, a new type of Hungarian culture, which is what we should be striving for." Even in later years he continued working to this end. From 1943 onwards he took part in the Committee for Pure Hungarian, set up by the Academy of Sciences; and in 1951 he presided over a conference of Hungarian philologists, and wrote a preface for Lajos Lőrincze's book, *Language and Life*. His teaching on this question may be summed up in his own words: "Correct speech is not a problem peculiar to philologists. It is a matter of public concern, of concern to us all."

This brings to an end our survey of Kodály's work as a teacher —a word which, in his case, is filled with a noble and generous significance. We have seen him as the Professor of Composition, as the teacher of youth, and as a man who in his writings and lectures is deeply and passionately concerned with the cultural advancement of his whole people. Always, his great learning and diverse interests have been combined with a readiness to assume practical responsibility and a willingness to undertake the most arduous tasks. As to the success of his endeavours, this is to be seen in the vitality of our contemporary composers, in the steady improvement in the teaching of music throughout our schools, and in the increasing numbers and far better training of our choirs. His own opinion of his achievements in this field he has expressed with characteristic modesty: "If I have succeeded in nothing else than in bringing the Hungarian town into closer contact with the Hungarian village, if only by a single step, my life will not have been wasted."

THE COMPOSER

Introduction

At the centre of Kodály's music, as of his other activities, is a striving towards greater synthesis, yet it remains essentially and predominantly Hungarian. As a composer he may be compared with an historian who has undertaken to write a universal history in his own language, for, in a very real sense, his music provides the first history of European music written in the Hungarian idiom. It is hardly an exaggeration to say his work is a summary of the great achievements of a thousand years of European art music, written, not in the common language of the post-romantic German composers, but in a contemporary Hungarian idiom created by himself. His rejection of that common language early in his career, which had involved renunciation of quick international success, sprang from a conviction that he was to express later in these words: "The works of art that exert the most powerful influence throughout the world as a whole, are those that express most fully the national characteristics of the artist. Since it is in such works that the highest individual creative power manifests itself, it follows that there is no individual originality which is not rooted in some kind of national originality."

The whole of his music is a practical realization of this belief, for however numerous its connexions with the great periods of European music, it still remains essentially Hungarian. Its roots reach back, on the one hand, through Debussy, Brahms, the Viennese classics, Bach and Palestrina to the Gregorian chant; on the other, through 19th century *verbunkos*[38] music, the Hungarian college music of the 18th century and the verse chronicles of the 16th century, to primitive Hungarian folk song: on the one hand, the mature complexity of the classics, on the other, a sparsity of art music but the tremendous raw material of folk music. Even a cursory examination of Kodály's antecedents warns us that we are faced with an unusual phenomenon. In contrast to those composers who may be regarded as "recapitulators"—those whose work is as a rule a summary of a single period, often of the few decades immediately preceding their own—Kodály's music unites the greatest achievements of several centuries and of two dissimilar cultures. It is his great achievement to have fused into a living unity elements that, if not irreconcilable, are at least extremely heterogeneous.

The aim he and Bartók set themselves was to condense into a single lifespan the whole experience of centuries of art music, for which Hungary, from her first primitive attempts at polyphony to the 20th century, was still dependent on Western Europe; and the difficulty of their task was aggravated by the fact that in Hungary, until their appearance on the scene, there had been practically no contact between genuine folk music and art music. In other countries, where development had been more normal, folk music had been a living experience for the earliest composers, influencing the higher art music throughout its development. The divergence of the two streams had not produced any abrupt cleavage: for example, to mention only two instances, throughout Europe melody in major keys remained characteristic of both, while the folk practice of *faux bourdon* could serve, as in England, as a natural foundation for the earliest experiments in polyphony. In Europe, in the course of centuries, there had arisen, despite the temporary hegemony of the various nations—perhaps, indeed, because of it—a continuously developing and homogeneous musical language, in comparison with which the particular native idioms revealed, at most, distinctions of dialect. In Hungary, by contrast, for the historical reasons already referred to, the rift between folk music and art music had almost proved fatal. The development of Hungarian music was marked, not by their salutary mutual influence, but by their seemingly irreconcilable contradiction.

It was for this reason, therefore, that in order to discover a firm basis on which to establish a national art music, Kodály and Bartók had first to collect, and then to analyze and study, the folk material that was already beginning to disappear. And what these two men accomplished in a single lifetime had elsewhere proved a work of several lifetimes (for example, in Germany, the popular melodies, first collected by Luther and a few of his associates, had to be elaborated by several generations, before they could attain their ultimate flowering in the music of Bach). Nor was this all. For, by summing up the past achievements of music in Europe and Hungary, they were only doing, so to speak, the work of their non-existent "predecessors." To catch up with the art music of the West was not enough: they had still to keep pace with its contemporary development. In order to appreciate Kodály's success in this vast endeavour, it is helpful to have some general conception of the musical outlook that confronted him, and of the part he played in transforming it.

A distinctive feature of all European music at the beginning of the century was the urge to experiment, the desire for originality at almost any price. Then, over a period that extended roughly from the production of Schoenberg's *Chamber Symphony* in 1906 to the formal proclamation of dodecaphony in 1925, what had begun as experiment began to harden into dogma. Throughout this period neo-romanticism and impressionism continued to play a part; the latter, though originating as a reaction against the former, proving to be in many respects merely an extension of it. It was the generation of composers born between 1874 and 1895 who initiated the new and more vigorous reaction, and whose experiments, aimed at the creation of a new musical language, centred around fundamental changes in the sphere of tonality and scale system; while in Germany and Austria, where the Wagnerian influence remained strongest, exaggerated chromaticism and linear thinking pointed the way to atonality and dodecaphony. The main representatives of this trend are Schoenberg, Hauer, Berg and Webern: other composers, centring around Hindemith, looked back to an earlier period, and eventually arrived at neo-classicism.

In many respects Stravinsky is at the opposite pole to the German school. In contrast to their sober style, in his music it is colour and orchestration that are primary, with the result that his thinking is of a more vertical kind. Moreover, with regard to tonality his standpoint is more conservative, for though he considerably enlarged the concept he never wholly abandoned it. In other directions, however, he is more advanced than they. It is rhythm, the second most characteristic feature of modern music, that constitutes the vital force in his work; while his use of eastern types of folk melody, and in general his use of folk music for something more than its mere colour effects, represents something qualitatively new in European music. In his second period, his work, like the early music of Prokofiev, is characterized by the striving towards neo-classicism.

In France, the situation confronting composers was an easier one. There, one of the achievements of impressionism had been the creation of a new musical idiom, susceptible of further development, which had already broken with traditional restrictions by its use of the pentatonic scale, harmonic tones and colour harmony. The French spirit, though freer from prejudice and more ready to accept what is new, is in other respects inclined to be traditionalist; and as we shall see later it is no accident that, of all European composers, it is precisely Honegger who in spirit is closest to Kodály.

Lastly, in this brief survey, mention must be made of those countries whose heritage of art music was relatively scanty. To appreciate the significance of folk music for these "border fortresses" it is sufficient to recall de Falla in Spain, Szymanowsky in Poland, in Czechoslovakia Janáček and Martinu, in Rumania Enescu; and by no means least, the two Hungarians, Bartók and Kodály.

To sum up, then, two main tendencies were to be distinguished in European music at the beginning of the century: the one strove to produce music that should be at once impersonal and thoroughly cosmopolitan in spirit (dodecaphony and neo-classicism); the other, exactly the opposite, sought to give ever more vigorous expression to national characteristics. Such, broadly speaking, was the situation confronting Kodály at the beginning of his career as a composer. In order to illustrate as vividly as possible both the nature of his contribution and the process by which his work entered into the mainstream of European music, we have attempted below to give a chronological summary of the principal musical developments during his lifetime.

1906. The first appearance of the pioneer works that, in contrast to the Wagnerian mammoth orchestras and Debussy's 'colour orchestration,' point the way towards soloistic treatment of the orchestra: Schoenberg's *Chamber Symphony*, and Kodály's earliest version of *Summer Evening*. In the same period, the earliest manifestation of Kodály's and Bartók's researches into folk music, the publication of twenty melodies in *Hungarian Folk Songs*.

1909. The Diaghilev Ballet makes its first appearance in Paris.—Production of Strauss's *Elektra*, further developing the characteristic features of Wagnerian music drama and carrying orchestral effects to extremes.— Completion of the first expressionistic work for the stage: Schoenberg's *Erwartung*.

1910. *Musique fauve*: Stravinsky's *Fire Bird*, with its violent orchestral colour and wild rhythms, establishes itself.—The end of Debussy's impressionist period, and the beginning of his neo-classical phase.

1911. Combination of impressionist technique with the strong colours of *musique fauve*, and greater attention to form and structure: Stravinsky's *Petrushka*.

1912. Under the influence of modern ballet, rhythm also begins to play a more dominant role in symphonic music.—Schoenberg's *Pierrot Lunaire*: the soloistic treatment of the orchestra, rather as in chamber music, represents a new milestone in the trend towards atonality.

1913. Stravinsky's "crisis": in the *Sacre du Printemps* he gives free rein to the primitive, organic elements of music.—With his *Glückliche Hand*, Schoenberg creates the type of opera characteristic of the movement towards abstraction.

1914-19. Development of neo-classicism (Ravel, Satie, Malipiero, and Pizzetti, as well as certain works by Stravinsky and Prokofiev).—Formation of the group of composers known as *Les Six*: Honegger, Milhaud, Auric, Poulenc, Durey and Tailleferre.—Jazz begins to exert an influence on art music: Cocteau's *Le Coq et l'Arlequin*.—A steadily increasing integration of music with the associated arts.

91

1920. Honegger and Hindemith engaged in reviving the classical sonata form; in his *Trio Serenade*, Kodály produces the most perfect example of this.—Thanks to individual and collective experiment, both conscious and unconscious, the theoretical bases of modern music are gradually established: but the search for form and classification still continues.

1921. To create a forum for experimentation, the Donaueschingen Festival is established.—Honegger composes his *King David*; Berg completes *Wozzeck*.

1923. Kodály composes the *Psalmus Hungaricus*.—The distinctive features of the two systems become increasingly clearly marked: development of dodecaphony towards complete atonality (Schoenberg, Webern); neo-classicist return to the music of the 17th and 18th centuries (Hindemith, Malipiero and others).

1925. The first formal proclamation of dodecaphony: Schoenberg's *Suite: Opus 25*.—Soviet music establishes itself in Western Europe, with works by Shostakovich and Shaporin.—Kodály's first children's choruses: *The Straw Guy* and *See, the Gypsy Munching Cheese*.

1927. Hindemith comes out publicly in favour of developing "national musical education."

1930-31. Rapid expansion of modern choral and oratorio music: works by Honegger, Hindemith, V. Williams, Walton and Stravinsky; Bartók's *Cantata Profana*, Kodály's *A Birthday Greeting*, *Mátra Pictures*, etc.

1935. Completion of Honegger's large-scale oratorio, *Jeanne d'Arc at the Stake*, for production on the stage.

1936. Kodály composes the *Te Deum of Budavár*; Orff, his *Carmina Burana*.—Such important contributions to instrumental music as Webern's *Variations*, Stravinsky's *Jeux de Cartes* and Bartók's *Music*.

1937. Publication of Hindemith's theoretical work, *Unterweisung im Tonsatz*, in which he applies his harmonic system to tonal, modal and atonal music alike. Poulenc and Milhaud turn to vocal lyricism, composing songs and cantatas thus confirming the stand already taken by Kodály.

1933-40. As a protest against fascism and the Nazis a number of composers emigrate: Schoenberg, Milhaud, Hindemith and Bartók.—Kodály chooses 'internal emigration,' expressing his protest by the revolutionary vigour of the variations for full orchestra on the folk song, *The Peacock*, which, as a choral work, had already been banned.

1940-45. A period of clarification and simplification; this tendency finding expression in works by Hindemith, Bartók, Stravinsky, Prokofiev and others.—Throughout the whole of Europe a growing interest in authentic folk music.

From this summary two main conclusions emerge with regard to Kodály's work. In the first place, he participated in the main developments of European music at those points where some healthy aspiration in the direction of humanism or classicism was either finding its earliest expression or reaching its climax.

This may be seen from the following examples: in 1906, when the composing of his *Summer Evening* coincided with the beginning of the movement against the use of oversized, disproportionately "antivocal" orchestras; in 1920 his *Serenade for Two Violins and Viola* made an important contribution to the revival of classical sonata form, all the more significant because of the increasingly dogmatic approach to new forms; in 1923 the *Psalmus Hungaricus* was written during the first great flowering of modern vocal music; in 1925, right at the beginning of the movement towards national musical education, he wrote his first children's choruses; and with the new development of chora music that took place in 1931, he produced his mixed choruses, culminating in the *Te Deum of Budavár* in 1936; and finally, in 1939, he joined the protest against fascism with what we have called his "internal emigration." Moreover, apart from these occasions when developments in Kodály's own work coincided with developments that were affecting European music as a whole, there were others when he himself led the way, as, for instance, his turn to vocal lyricism in 1937; or again, in 1940, when he set the example for greater simplification with his insistence on tonality, the importance of melody and of authentic folk song.

In the second place, it is clear that Kodály held aloof from the main stream of European music during those periods that were characterized by experiment for the sake of experiment. He was not among those adherents of the dodecaphonic system who, ignoring the demands of the public, became increasingly abstract; nor was he one of those neo-classicists whose works were tending to become little more than stylistic exercises. He refused to allow his aesthetic principles to become rigid dogmas: on the one hand, because his classicism was more instinctive, more comprehensive than what is implied in neo-classicism; on the other, because the hyper-chromatic, atonal features of dodecaphony and the morbidly overheated character of expressionism, seeking refuge in a world of glittering speculation, were, in their profound anti-humanism, essentially alien to his own personality and to the spirit of folk music as well.

Thus, in the development of his work, we see him at times participating in international movements, at times himself determining their direction; and, yet again, going his own way, ignoring experiments which, however daring, strike him as being fruitless. Of course, the path he chose, and the moment of choice, throw a significant light on the nature of his creative gifts. But that choice was never made solely in terms of his own creative demands or personal inclinations, it was also determined by his whole ethical outlook, his feeling of responsibility to his people and of duty to his country.

Having thus briefly indicated the nature of Kodály's contribution to the history of 20th century music, we come now to the appreciation of his artistic achievement. But before proceeding to the analysis of individual works, we feel it may be of use to attempt some general account of his style; of its main components, particularly in the sphere of melody and harmony. From what has already been said it is clear that a distinctive feature of it is that it is organic, and organic in a two-fold sense. In the first place it has a living connexion not only with the past, but also, through the influence it has exerted on the latest Hungarian music, with the future. And in the second place, there is, within each of his individual works, an organic relationship between the various parts that constitutes a living and homogeneous unity.

With regard to his historical antecedents, we have already mentioned Debussy, Brahms, the Viennese classics, Bach, Palestrina and the Gregorian chant. As with Palestrina, it is the human voice that first inspires Kodály; and the two masters are related, too, in their use of vocal polyphony. As one would expect, this kinship finds expression rather in the spiritual depths of their work than in its external features, most clearly of all perhaps, at the beginning of the Sanctus in the *Missa Brevis*. In his use of another, baroque, type of polyphony Kodály derives from Bach. The tremendous massed choruses of *Jesus and the Traders*, the outstanding 20th century choral masterpiece, is clearly related to the great *Passions*. And a further reminiscence of Bach may also be noted in the same work, where the symbolism of the music is closely linked with the words; as for example in the passage beginning, "And braiding a whip from rope," where the sinuously interwoven semi-quaver figures seem almost to convey the quality of rope. From the formal point of view, yet another obvious link between the work of Kodály and the music of the baroque period is the way in which, in his monumental *Concerto*, he fills the old *concerto grosso* form with an entirely new content.

As for the spirit of Viennese classicism, its influence on Kodály's work may be seen in his brilliant contemporary adaptation of such basic musical forms as the sonata, the three-part song, the rondo and variations. His highly developed feeling for proportion and his determination to preserve tonality, characteristic of both his early and mature styles, are not specifically Viennese, but stem from a more comprehensively classical outlook. (We use the word tonality in its broadest sense, to include the new scale system as well as the fields of melody and harmony.) As Bartók said in an article he wrote in 1921 "On

Modern Hungarian Music": "Kodály has no connexion whatsoever with the new atonal, bitonal and polytonal types of music. The guiding principle of all his work is still a balanced tonality. Yet he speaks, in a language that is itself new, of things that hitherto have not been spoken of; thus proving that the principle of tonality is still a legitimate one."

It is only in his early works that we find traces of the romantic style. In the works of his maturity, only the faintest echo of this period is to be heard in the harmony, as for example in the extreme use of the third-changing relationship, serving primarily to underline the meaning of the text, which is to be found in the mixed chorus, *Evening*, and elsewhere. Another example is the mixture of basic harmonies, familiar to us from the music of Schubert, that occurs at the opening of the *Te Deum*, where, in contrast to the dominant-tonic–dominant-tonic of the melody–may be heard a dominant-subdominant-tonic-dominant harmony. And yet another romantic echo is the improvising style of instrumentalization that Kodály is so fond of; though, as this is also characteristic of the performance of instrumental folk music, it is to this, perhaps, that we should attribute the influence.

When we look for evidence of the most immediate of his stylistic antecedents, French impressionism, we find it mainly in his harmonic and scale systems, although, unlike Debussy, Kodály never strives to attain pure colour effects by his use of mixtures, the combination of chords and chromatic progressions, but always subordinates these to the demands of his melodic invention.

Yet though these historical European influences undoubtedly helped to form Kodály's style, they were less significant than that other heritage, less easily to be distinguished, the heritage of Hungarian folk music and Hungarian art music, the synthesis of which is the crowning achievement of Kodály's art. Of the comparatively few examples of the latter that were extant, it was perhaps the melodic type of songs from the 16th century verse chronicles and the rhythms of 19th century *verbunkos* music that Kodály found most stimulating. But of all the influences that affected his style Hungarian folk music was far and away the most important, and particularly those examples of it, only recently discovered, that belong to the most primitive level: the four-line songs, using the pentatonic scale with no semitones, constructed on a system of fifth-transposition.[39] This influence may be noted in those characteristic melodic phrases in which he frequently makes use of progressions of fourths; in his scale system (though here he draws on the modal scales connected with Gregorian plain-song, as well as the pentatonic scale); and in his rhythms, as is shown by the frequent occurrence in his work of *parlandos* and *rubatos*. Furthermore, the characteristic line construction of these songs becomes for him a basic formal principle; while the recurrent sequential structure in his music is essentially derived from their construction on a system of fifth-transposition. Indeed, it is through his brilliant exploitation of the harmonic possibilities inherent in the ancient monophonic folk song (with the addition of pentatonic tonics, dominants, etc.), that Kodály succeeded in establishing the distinctive harmony of modern polyphonic art music. And, lastly, the fact that with folk music its mode of presentation is an integral part of the music, with the result that it is, and must be, continually subject to variation, has clearly had an important bearing on the development of Kodály's improvisational instrumental style. Here, once again, we may usefully refer to Bartók. In an article written in 1931, discussing the various ways in which folk music had influenced art music, he said that sometimes composers had simply introduced a folk melody into their own work, either in its original form, or with slight modifications; sometimes they had composed imitation folk melodies and developed them in the same manner. But, he went on, far the most significant form this influence could take was when a composer, without either appropriating or imitating folk melodies, wrote in such a way "that his music created the same atmosphere as folk music. For only then could he be said to have really learned the musical dialect of the peasants, only then could he be as much at home with it as a poet is with his native tongue... And of all Hungarian composers, it is Kodály whose work provides the supreme examples of this." And elsewhere he made the same point even more emphatically. "If I were asked in whose music is the spirit of Hungary most perfectly embodied," he wrote, "I would reply, in Kodály's. His music is, indeed, a profession of faith in the spirit of Hungary. Objectively, this may be explained by the fact that his work as a composer is exclusively rooted in the soil of Hungarian folk music. But, subjectively, it is due to Kodály's unwavering faith in the creative strength of his people, and his confidence in their future."

That Kodály's music is deeply, if not 'exclusively,' rooted in folk music is, of course, beyond question. Part of it, indeed, is a polyphonic elaboration of monophonic folk song: but even the most individual and personal part of his work is conceived in the spirit of folk song. And this double aspect is perfectly natural. For folk music is, on the one hand, a completely integrated, classically mature, collective art form, only awaiting, so to speak, the arrival of polyphony; while, on the other, it may be regarded as the raw material of music, which has taken shape over the centuries, independently of, and largely prior to, the development of formally organized western music; and which, broken down into its elements, can serve as the basis for a new style of art music.

Nothing could be more misleading, however, than to attempt to represent Kodály's style as simply the sum of the various aspects of it that we have been discussing. Certainly it is one of his most distinctive characteristics that he has

The First Page of the Manuscript of *Psalmus Hungaricus*

Programme for the First Performance of the *Spinning-Room* Abroad (Milan, 1933)

succeeded in integrating so many, and such widely diversified, elements of style—in a way that is unique in the 20th century, and, quite possibly, in the whole history of music. And this could only have been achieved by a composer with Kodály's breadth of vision and profound scholarship. But, over and above all this, it is his own imaginative power that enables him to combine all these varied components in such a way as to produce the specific and original musical language that we recognize as "the Kodály style."

If we examine this first from the point of view of his melody, what is immediately striking is the dissimilarity in this respect between the vocal and instrumental works. In the vocal works, it is primarily the text that determines the melodic character: the scale system, the dynamics and rhythm, in polyphonic compositions the texture and the treatment of the accompaniment, whether instrumental or orchestral. In general, the body of the melodies is of a diatonic minor character with pentatonic phrases, and a sparing use of chromaticism in accordance with the demands of the text. To attempt to reduce them to any system of classification would be merely arbitrary, for the fact is that there are as many types of melody as there are texts. With regard to the character of his instrumental melodies, however, the position is different: for while, on the one hand, they are not restricted by the limitations of the singing voice, on the other, being freed from the compulsion to diversity imposed by the text, they tend to be more homogeneous and therefore lend themselves more readily to classification.

Particularly characteristic of Kodály is the free, improvising melodic treatment that we find in a considerable group of his instrumental works, of which there is a good example in the introductory bars of the third movement of the *Duo:*

1

Duo (Op.7): III. 1-5.
Maestoso e largamente, ma non troppo lento

This type of melody differs fundamentally from the vocal melodies, which, even where the text is in prose, have a linear, periodic, architectonic and entirely melodic structure. The improvising style is also formal, with its own inner proportions, yet its character and effect are entirely different, and very typical. Its most distinctive features are: the start on a long note falling on an accented beat, introducing a slow motive of vocal style, usually pentatonic in character; which is then developed instrumentally, accelerating in speed, and ornamentally providing a development, as it were, of the opening phrases. He does not develop this into a melody, but either expands and develops its scope, as in the *Duo*, or, on the contrary, uses it to fill in the spaces of the originally wider ranges as in the *lassú* (meaning slow) of the *Second String Quartet:*

2
Second String Quartet (Op. 10) : II, Opening Bars.
Andante. Quasi recit.

The other main type of instrumental melody, often encountered in the quick last movements, is reminiscent of the stereotyped rhythms and repetitive melodic phrases that are familiar from Hungarian children's songs and counting-out songs, for instance this passage from the second movement of the *Sonata for 'Cello and Piano:*

3
Sonata for 'Cello and Piano (Op. 4) : II, Opening Bars.
Allegro con spirito

In addition to these two principal types, however, the range of his instrumental melodies is extremely varied, extending from the slow, *rubato* folk-song elaborations to the *verbunkos* music of *Háry János*, from almost monotonous recitative to extravagant flourishes.

In his use of harmony, though in many respects following the French impressionists, Kodály differs from them in that it is always his soaring melodic invention that is the decisive factor. Indeed, in the final analysis, it will be found that his harmony is always subordinate to, and determined by, the melody. Drawing upon the whole range of scale systems—from the most natural pentatonic, overtone and modal scales to the whole-tone system, which defies the laws, not only of acoustics but also of consecutive fifths—he derives from them, in the light of the almost unlimited 20th century conception of consonance, his own specific harmony; creating harmonies simultaneously from the successive melodic figures. Thus his peculiar pentatonic harmonies are created from the pentatonic Hungarian folk songs, in the same way that the

98

major-minor harmonies of western music are derived from the troubadour songs and other monophonic melodies.

A distinctive feature of his treatment of chords is his use of 'colour' notes—auxiliary notes, which he attaches to one or more notes of a conventionally constructed chord, in such a way that the notes are not sounded in sequence, but simultaneously. Here the auxiliary notes are not restricted to intervals of a second, but are extended to intervals of a third, and even a fourth, and are generally left unresolved. Moreover, he has further developed the conventional construction of chords in thirds: in addition to chords of the seventh and ninth, as used hitherto, chords of elevenths and thirteenths, i. e., consisting of six and seven notes, frequently occur. And lastly, he makes as much use of harmonies built on fourths and seconds as of those built on thirds.

Another significant feature of his harmonic style is his use of the mixture based on a development of *faux bourdon* technique, with parallel seconds, fourths and sevenths. We find two main types of mixture in his works: in one type, the chords preserve the structure of the first, but retain the tonality; in the second type, the intervals of the first chord are exactly repeated. Sometimes the mixture follows the melody, and its significance is simply melodic-harmonic; sometimes it serves to modulate, and, by affecting the structure, has a form-creating role and yet again it provides atmosphere by oscillating between the chords.

Also characteristic is the way Kodály sometimes harmonizes by attaching chords belonging to one degree of the scale to another degree (thus giving them a different tonal function), so that the chord becomes, as it were, "suspended." Or, again, he will change a dominant seventh chord enharmonically into a German sixth chord, in this way releasing the dominant seventh chord from its natural function and re-interpreting it as a subdominant.

Thus Kodály's harmony sometimes completely supports the melody, as the harmonic accompaniment derived from it; sometimes it achieves greater independence, except at those points of special structural importance where he uses a kind of pedal-point. Both types are clearly illustrated on page 100, in a passage from the third movement of the *Duo*.

The essence of this apparent independence of melody and harmony lies in the "auxiliary melody" developed from the auxiliary note (e. g. the opening melody of the mixed chorus, *Evening*), which recalls the "pseudo-polyphony" of Bach's chorales. Here the structure is homophonic. But though between the turning-points the various voices pursue their own way, with the result that almost any kind of dissonance may occur, such is the logic of their development that, at the turning-points, all the voices come together into a con-

7*

4

Duo (Op. 7) : III, 19-51 after ⑥

Poco meno mosso

sonance. This is why, taken as a whole, Kodály's harmony has a classical quality: he never introduces dissonances merely for their own sake, but always in response to the inner logic of his musical imagination. The major triad, so rarely heard in contemporary music, he uses frequently (here, again, sometimes independently of the melody), for his primary concern is always to achieve harmonies that are acoustically perfect, or perhaps more correctly, that sound well. And indeed, for a composer determined to write for the widest public and to help in the development of their taste, this was the only path open to him.

We shall have more to say about Kodály's rhythms and forms in connexion with particular works, but it may be worth mentioning at this point one or two general characteristics. Apart from his admirable feeling for balance and proportion, it will be found that, whereas in the vocal works the form is for the most part determined by the words, in the instrumental music the structure is derived from classical models, though as a rule he makes use, not of one particular form, but rather of a mixture of several. In his treatment of

repeats and *reprises*, their form is never identical, but always varied or modified. Typical of his manner of developing his themes are: a more or less closed
line construction, periodization, transpositions that are reminiscent of the
repetitions at a different pitch typical of folk song, and an overall recognition
of the importance homophonic or polyphonic texture. He delights in using the
classical four-part form, in which, after two closed or static parts, comes a
dynamic third part which, by "remaining open," so to speak, leads on into
the final closed section. This, with repeated exposition, is the structure of the
classical sonata form; but, equally, it is typical of the simplest Hungarian folk
songs. And it will be found that this AABA principle prevails not only in
Kodály's sonata movements, but also in the opening theme of the *Te Deum*
and in other works.

The fact that this identical principle is to be found in the most highly
developed art music of Western Europe, as well as in the simplest folk songs
of eastern origin, brings us back to what we said earlier about Kodály's
"striving to achieve a synthesis," about his gifts as a "summarizer." But, of
course, it must be realized that such a synthesis is not to be attained simply by
taking over stylistic elements from other epochs or other composers. Rather,
it is the result of a spiritual inter-penetration that enables an artist of one
epoch to identify himself with the achievements of another. It was this that
enabled Kodály, and Bartók, to establish a miraculous unity between ancient
melody and modern harmony, between the collective will and the individual
consciousness, between folk music and art music—the great synthesis of the
music of Hungary with the music of Europe. At the basis of his achievement
is the fact that his art is at once classical and humanist. Amidst the storm of
violently conflicting opinions he never lost his nobility of purpose, and in an
era often distinguished by its inhumanity he still retained his love of his fellow
men.

Chamber Music and Orchestral Works

The following chapters are in no sense intended as an exhaustive set of
programme notes to Kodály's works. Their aim is rather to illustrate, by
reference to characteristic examples of their use, the distinctive features of
his style that we have been discussing. The bulk of his chamber music was
written in the years 1905 to 1920, and therefore, despite its maturity and very
considerable merits, belongs to the period of his youth, when his main purpose
was the perfecting of his technique in preparation for more testing achievements. It was here that he experimented in the development of that instrumental style which, almost at the end of this period, attained its first full

101

expression in the *Psalmus Hungaricus*. Prior to this (if we leave out of account his childhood attempts), he only completed one orchestral work, the first draft of *Summer Evening;* and even this still bears the characteristics of chamber music. Subsequently he composed but little chamber music, and then almost invariably in the form of transcriptions. (As we shall see later, in the field of vocal music, the songs fulfil a similar function.) Both the beginning and the end of the period are marked by masterpieces, the *Adagio* and the *Serenade for Two Violins and Viola*—two works which, though unmistakably by the same composer, nevertheless display the most profound differences. Writing in 1932, that is to say after the *Psalmus Hungaricus, Háry János* and the *Dances of Marosszék,* Kodály himself said of the *Adagio:* "Up to now it has proved to be the most popular of my works. None of my other music has been performed so frequently; and indeed there are some radio programmes where it is still featured every week. Since it dates from a time when as yet I knew nothing about folk music—or at least, nothing more than such superficial notions of it as were then current—it would be possible to deduce from it what kind of music I should have written if there had been no folk music, or if I had never visited the country districts and had therefore failed to discover it... There is no trace of Hungarian folk music in the *Adagio*... It is written in a fluent, fairly lucid, internationally comprehensible style... and had I continued to write like this I should have found success easier of achievement."

The piece is in three-part form, having a coda that is developed out of the middle open episode. In its melodic line and the accompaniment of the opening theme, the influence of the romantic masters is apparent; but its melodic structure—AABA$_\text{v}$—already has something in common with the structure of folk song. In the middle episode the second statement of the theme, by sequence, comes as a surprise:

5

Adagio for Violin and Piano: Più andante, 2-9.

Both the modulation and the internal structure are typical Kodály. And there are a number of other features characteristic of his later style; for instance, the instrumental type of melody at the end of the episode; the close (composed, as it were, of overtones) on a dominant seventh, that changes enharmonically into a German sixth chord which is resolved; the sequential repetition of the closing motive, leading to the *reprise;* and the changes that occur in the *reprise.* Interesting, also, is the end of the work: the middle episode returns, again with a modulation, but after a few bars it breaks up into a large-scale coda, the tempo accelerating to a climax, when it breaks off and gradually disappears into oblivion. Consider the final bars:

6
Idem, Closing Bars.

It begins with a motive composed of whole tones, descending and growing gradually slower, in a manner that recalls Debussy. Beneath this theme is a dominant seventh chord (unfunctional in character), that changes enharmonically into German sixth, in a manner that was later to become typical of Kodály's style. Then, at the end of the fourth bar, appears a turn of a fourth, typical of folk song, and the work closes with a variation on this figure, the melody of which is completely pentatonic, while its underlying harmony, recalling Liszt's later style, consists of a series of descending major triads.

103

A significant stage in Kodály's development is marked by the *Nine Pieces for Piano*, dating from 1909, for here the influence of folk song is indubitable, its melodic figures and rhythmic formulae occurring, no longer by chance, but as the result of serious study. Indeed, although other influences still exert almost equal weight, it is clear that Kodály was here beginning to use certain elements of folk music experimentally for the fashioning of his unique musical language.

While each of these beautifully written little works is inspired by a different idea, the exposition of which determines their form, they all display a new kind of piano technique and are characterized by the free use of rhythmic and harmonic *ostinatos*. The first of them, the *Lento*, with its atmosphere of suffering and resignation, consists of two four-line strophes, in two-part form. Its basic idea is a perfect fifth. This is the framework for the two-bar motive, from the variations on which the strophe is constructed; while the series of descending mixtures of fifths in the accompaniment forms its modulatory basis.

The brilliantly written third piece, after a slow, quiet start, gradually accelerates to a passionate climax, and then once again subsides. The modal melody is heard beneath a sextolet *ostinato* figure in the accompaniment, that reminds one of Liszt's piano technique. Here, the fundamental musical ideas are an easy transition between modes belonging to the same scale system, the creeping character of the modal melody without a leading note, the possibility of "hetero-modality" in melody and accompaniment; and, as an extension of this, the possibility of contrasting the modal character of the principal intervals of the melody—perfect fourths and fifths—with the predominantly Lydian, tritonal accompaniment. Here is the beginning of the accompaniment and the melody:

7

Nine Pieces for Piano (Op. 3): No. 3, 1-2.

Andante *(l'accompagnement sans rigueur, poco rubato)*

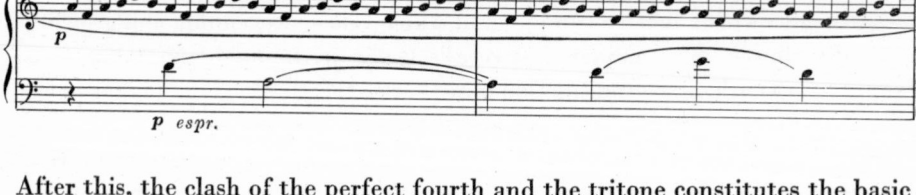

After this, the clash of the perfect fourth and the tritone constitutes the basic conflict, which culminates in the outburst of the augmented fourth (fortissimo) at the end of the coda-like third part.

The fifth piece, the *Furioso*, is a kind of two-part toccata, in which the central idea is a single chord, constructed of a major and a minor second and a major third. The *ostinato*-like vibration of this chord over the two-line semi-folk song and the frequent organ pedal-points are particularly effective. And it is interesting to note how Kodály, in contrast to the folk-song theme, introduces elements usually foreign to him: e. g. the Locrian mode, the use of the augmented fourth, the distuned tonic, and the run in major thirds on the dominant. However, towards the end of the piece, as though by way of reminder, a characteristic pentatonic closing line once again makes its appearance.

In the remaining pieces in the series (apart from No. 8, where the scintillating colour effects derive from French sources), the influence of folk music is even more clearly discernible. Of them all, it is perhaps the sad and plaintive No. 6 that most unmistakably bears the imprint of Kodály's mature style, with its folk-song-like theme supported by an accompaniment sometimes in triplets, sometimes syncopated, and sometimes *ostinato*. No. 7 consists of a gay folk-dance theme with two variations and a coda. And, finally, the *Allegro commodo, burlesco* brings the series to an effective close with a display of exuberant humour.

The *Seven Pieces for Piano* (Op. 11) mark a further stage in Kodály's technical experiments. Of these all, except the third, which was written in 1910, belong to the year 1917-18. The mood of this early piece, which bears as epigraph the line from Verlaine, *Il pleure dans mon coeur comme il pleut sur la ville*, is typical of the brooding melancholy that gives unity to the work as a whole. But while in this case, as one would expect, the influence of French impressionism is still strong, the other pieces are remarkable for their musical material and technical diversity. The first, *Lento*, with its melody formed from a combination of the whole-tone and chromatic systems, creates an almost *pointilliste* effect, in sharp contrast to the second, *Székely Lament*. In this piece, written in three parts, the melodic material is pure pentatony, and the harmonies are the pentatonic harmonies characteristic of folk song. Among its notable features are, firstly, the dissonant middle section, which opens a semitone higher, with harmonies distuned from pentatonic harmonies (auxiliary chords rendered dissonant by the number of auxiliary notes); and, secondly, the "unfolding," so to speak, of the third strophe, which returns to the fundamental key on the pentatonic dominant. Here Kodály does not follow the melody from note to note, but only in its descending line, until it returns to its starting-point, the whole-tone character gradually giving way to pentatonic consonance:

8

Seven Pieces for Piano (Op. 11): No. 2, Closing Bars.

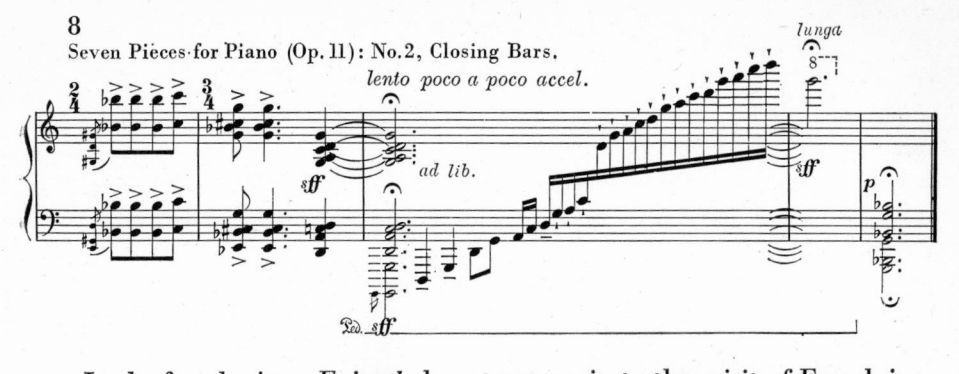

In the fourth piece, *Epitaph*, he returns again to the spirit of French impressionism; but the fifth, with its expansive pentatonic melody, and the genuinely folk-type melodies of the two last pieces, are prophetic of his mature style.

But, despite the value of these piano works, it was in the chamber music written for strings that Kodály carried out his most vital instrumental experiments. Already in the *First String Quartet (Op. 2)*, completed in 1909—a work that may almost be regarded as the precursor of his great orchestral folk-song variation, *The Peacock*—he based his music for the first time on elements entirely derived from folk music. Here is the first line of the folk song that constitutes the basis for the melodic material of the work and the character variations that occur in the different movements:

9

First String Quartet (Op. 2): Opening Bars & Variations.

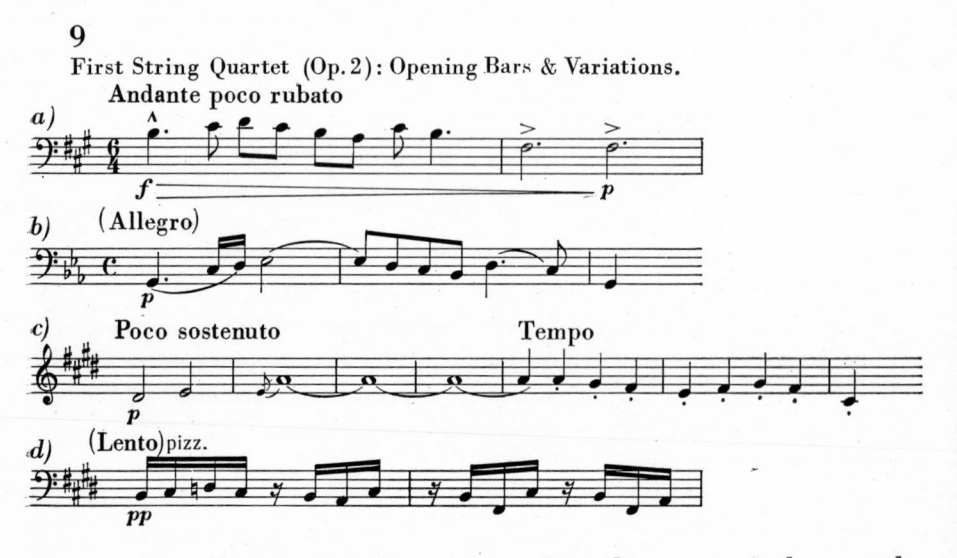

In addition to the melodic figures, the orchestral treatment is also strongly influenced by folk music; while the fresh and original harmonies (apart from the introduction of elements so foreign to folk music as the use of intervals of augmented fourths) stem from the interaction of independent voices, and, throughout, carry conviction. From the formal point of view, the first movement, which resembles a sonata, is followed by a slow kind of *fugato* movement, then by a fast and dynamic trio-type piece, and lastly by a finale, which introduces a number of variations. The principal theme of the finale consists of a simple major melody, harmonized in accordance with classical rules. The variations are original and imaginative; and one of them, the exceptionally brilliant *Allegretto* in 5/8 time, was contributed by Kodály's wife.

The next example of chamber music, the *Sonata for 'Cello and Piano* (Op. 4), written in 1909-10, is derived entirely from folk music. This is made clear by the C sharp-F sharp-G sharp-C sharp signature at the beginning, by the fact that the melody is constructed on a series of fourths, by the *rubato*, and by the improvisational style of instrumentalization in the opening movement, the *Fantasia*. This Fantasia is repeated at the end of the second movement, which is otherwise of regular sonata form, and in this way a formal unity is achieved of a higher order than the mere unity of motives in the *First String Quartet*. The sense of balance and unity is further enhanced by the symmetrical key structure—the sonata movement, which ends in key of G, being preceded by an F sharp, which is later repeated, while sections in keys with a number of flats are counterbalanced by others in keys with a number of sharps.

The four further examples of chamber music we have to consider in many respects constitute a single group, despite their considerable diversity. Written in the period 1914 to 1920, all four of them—the *Duo for Violin and 'Cello* (Op. 7), the *Sonata for 'Cello Solo* (Op. 8), the *Second String Quartet* (Op. 10), and the *Trio Serenade* (Op. 12)—are evidence that Kodály was no longer feeling his way, but had achieved a mature personal style and was already looking ahead to the writing of orchestral works. Moreover, in addition to having a number of formal features in common, all four works are written exclusively for string instruments.

In the construction of the *Duo* most of the elements are familiar, having already been employed earlier, and the originality of the work is largely attributable to the unusual combination of instruments and to the new possibilities of sound thus provided. In a richly imaginative way, Kodály exploits the similar technical capabilities of the two instruments—the fact that, while both are suitable for performing the same kind of melodic figures, their difference of tone ensures diversity. (One has only to think of the many questions and responses and their harmonious blending, or of the various imitations, and the way they are drawn together in unison passages.) Throughout the major part of the work *rubato* instrumental folk themes are predominant, though in the *Presto* of the final movement a children's song is introduced, with its driving *ostinato* and rigidly disciplined rhythm. Apart from their familiar use instead of modulations, sequences and ornamental elements abound throughout the *Duo*. In the midst of the surging pentatonic melodies in the trio of the finale the only firm tonality introduced is that which is based on the distance of the tritone (*see* 4th musical illustration p. 100).

The structure of this work is also interesting. The first movement is in regular sonata form. Characteristically the principal theme starts on the pentatonic minor seventh (C in a strongly established D tonality); and the typically folk, four-line form at the beginning is continued, from the third line onwards, with a kind of improvising instrumental style:

10

Duo (Op. 7) : I, 1-5.

Allegro serioso, non troppo

The second movement might be described as a sonata loosened into a fantasia, with a double-fugue-like principal theme and strongly contrasted reprise:

11

Idem : II, 1-10.

Adagio

(Sections A and B of this theme recur later in the form of a simultaneous double fugue.)

The third movement combines a slow introduction, a trio-like form and a coda, with the theme of the second movement being repeated in the last bars of the introduction as though this were an extension of the second movement. The coda, which provides an effective close, is developed out of the clattering semi-quavers of the trio *ostinato*.

With the *Sonata for 'Cello Solo*, Kodály once again showed himself to be a pioneer, for apart from three *Suites* by Max Reger,[40] this was the first major unaccompanied work for 'cello since Bach; though shortly afterwards Hindemith was to compose others. Speaking of the *Sonata* in an article, "The New Music of Hungary," written in 1921, Bartók said: "No other composer has written music that is at all similar to this type of work—least of all Reger, with his pale imitations of Bach. Here Kodály is expressing, with the simplest possible technical means, ideas that are entirely original. It is precisely the complexity of the problem that offered him the opportunity of creating an original and unusual style, with its surprising effects of vocal type; though quite apart from these effects the musical value of the work is brilliantly apparent."

An interesting feature of the *Sonata* is that here Kodály revives the use of scordatura, as practised in the 17th and 18th centuries, which calls for the re-tuning of the two lower strings from C-G to B-F sharp. And, also for the first time, he displays an amazing virtuosity, doubtless as a result of his having to rely on the solo instrument. Discarding the classical structure and configurations in this work, he uses in their place those original figures and other musical devices with which he had experimented in his earlier chamber works. Though the unity of the form as a whole is sustained by the fact that its themes are derived from a common source, the individual movements differ considerably from each other—from the drama of the first movement, through the soaring melodies of the second, to the dazzling virtuosity of the third.

In the *Second String Quartet* what comes as a surprise, even to those already familiar with the development of Kodály's style, is the profound identification he achieves between his own personal utterance and the spirit of folk music. Here the essence of folk song is transmuted into the stylistic elements of an art music perfectly adapted to classical form, in a way that is only possible for a composer to whom folk music has become his mother tongue. The first movement, with its atmosphere of gloom, contains within itself in condensed form the great ABA structure of the *Sonata for 'Cello and Piano* (fantasia-sonata-fantasia *reprise*), and once again the introduction recurs at the end of the movement to form a bridge. The second movement recalls the final movement of the *Duo*, though here the introduction with its moderate tempo is not a development of, but rather a substitution for, the slow movement, which in this case is omitted. Gradually the distinctive syncopated rhythm of one of the themes of what is, in fact, the finale (the disguised third movement), is woven into the texture of the music; and, indeed, this same theme, as though unable to restrain itself, has already been heard in the slow introduction.

The final movement, the *Allegro*, is in sonata form, though without a development section; and after what one at first senses to be the close of the exposition, a new group of closing themes is introduced, built in like a trio, which itself constitutes a small, compact two-part form. Then follows a *reprise*, diversified by a number of short imitations (by way of development), and a coda consisting of a trio-like group of closing themes. The way in which the content of this movement is condensed is most striking. With typical prodigality Kodály pours forth a succession of themes, of distinctive and exquisite beauty—ample proof of his rich melodic invention:

12
Second String Quartet (Op. 10) : II, Themes of Finale.

This spirited, dance-like finale is also significant from the point of view of form, because, with its peculiar combination of sonata, sonata-rondo, trio and two- and three-part forms, it already foreshadows the creative, unifying formal principle that Kodály was later to assert most perfectly in the *Te Deum*.

110

The culminating achievement of his chamber music period, however—is the *Serenade for Two Violins and Viola.* Here, in contrast to the *Duo,* he makes use of closely related instruments, two violins and a viola; and one of the chief merits of this captivating and high-spirited work is the lustrous purity and resonance achieved by the strings. As regards melody and harmony, it represents the culmination of those distinctive feature that had been maturing in his earlier works. Where it transcends them is, above all, in the more organic unity of its thematic structure and its clearer arrangement of key relationship. Here, the key relationships are organically linked, not simply juxtaposed as in the classical sonata. For example, the first movement begins in the dominant and returns to the tonic; the second starts in the sub-dominant, returns to the dominant and ends on the tonic. Later, he was again to make use of this formal unification by means of classical key relationships in the introduction to the *Psalmus Hungaricus.*

Regarded purely in terms of form, the structure of the work is easy to follow. After a first movement in sonata form, the second is constructed on the principle, AABA, with the second theme constituting a reference back to the main theme of the previous movement. Then comes the final movement, which is a still further development of the kind of "combination" already familiar from the *Duo* and the *Second String Quartet.* But here, as the title is perhaps intended to suggest, it is not merely a question of form: for if we experience the musical content of the work more deeply, a moving story unfolds itself.

At the start, we hear three musicians, playing a serenade beneath a woman's window (clearly, the unconventional, swiftly-moving $^3/_4$ theme of the first movement, with the flurrying semi-quavers *ostinato,* is inspired by a serenade):

13
Serenade (Op. 12) : I, 1-5.

Then comes a song from the lover (its exceptionally expressive melody fulfilling all the requirements of the contrasting theme of the sonata); while the alternation between the voices of the musicians and the lover, heard now separately, now together, complies strictly with the rules of the development and the *reprise*. The second movement opens with a dialogue between the lover (viola) and his mistress (first violin), while the tremolos of the second violin suggest the atmosphere of night. To the lover's pleading the woman replies with laughter, coyness gradually turning into passionate rejection:

14
Idem : II, 1-11.

At this point, the lover dismisses the musicians (this is where the principal theme of the first movement, the serenade motif, is repeated); whereupon the woman relents, and it is now the man who laughs. (Here, again, the clever alternation of the themes of violin and viola comply with the strict demands of form.) Lastly, the third movement confirms the understanding between lover and mistress, the light-hearted banter between viola and violin developing into a song of satisfied love; and the tale is brought to an end with an invigorating dance.

This work, with its classical clarity of structure and sense of proportion, and with its wealth of melodic invention, is undoubtedly one of the masterpieces of 20th century chamber music.

*

Just as most of Kodály's chamber music was written between 1905 and 1920, so too a considerable number, though not all, of his orchestral works belong to the period 1923 to 1939. Here, again, both the beginning and end of the period are marked by masterpieces, the *Psalmus Hungaricus* and *The*

112

Kodály with the Swiss Conductor Ansermet

Kodály with some of his Former Pupils
(Left to right Gyula Kertész, Kodály, Iván Engel, Tibor Serly,
Mátyás Seiber, István Szelényi, Jenő Ádám, Lajos Bárdos,
Mihály Szigeti, György Kerényi

Kodály Conducting in Moscow (1947)

Peacock; though because of the importance of the vocal parts, both solo and choral, in the first of these, we shall not be discussing it here but later on, with its companion pieces, the *Te Deum* and *Missa Brevis.*

In the case of *Summer Evening,* the first of the orchestral works we have to consider, though there was an earlier version dating back to 1906 which, in its original form, was only performed twice, the present version was written in 1929, at the instance of Toscanini, and is now established as a favourite programme piece. As no score of the 1906 version is available, any comparison between the two can only be by inference. Kodály himself, in a brief introductory note written in 1930, said: "The original conception of timbre remains unchanged; and the instruments, too, are the same, save for the omission of a third horn. While the musical treatment is similar, in the new version it is more in accordance with the acoustical laws laid down by Chladni." In view of this, and from what we know of Kodály's early style, it seems probable that the revision was concerned primarily with the formal aspect of the work, and possibly with the kind of harmonization employed. Certainly the 1930 version is notable for its use of the sonata form, for the plasticity of its themes and its classical sense of proportion. At the same time, with regard to the melodic material used, the lyrically subjective character of the work and its orchestration, the later work appears to have remained practically unchanged—already, in 1906, the orchestration had been considered a revolutionary innovation. Though his chamber music of this period still retained several romantic features, here, in his first large-scale orchestral work, Kodály turned his back on the late romantic predilection for monstrous orchestras and relied for what he had to say on a small chamber orchestra. But while there are no percussion instruments in *Summer Evening,* and while the brass is represented only by horns, on the other hand the woodwind plays an important part.

The principal theme is announced by the *Cor Anglais:*

15
Summer Evening : 1-7.
Andante assai
a) Cor. ingl.

p *espr.*

And the melody is developed antiphonally by the solo instrument, the strings and the woodwind. In the 63rd bar, again on the *Cor Anglais,* the outline appears, reduced to pure pentatony:

Idem: 63.

b) Cor. ingl.

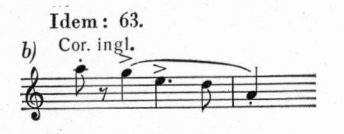

The second subject is structurally related to *The Peacock*. First the major variant is heard in the woodwind and strings:

16

Idem: 109-117.

a)

And this is later interwoven with a series of pentatonic figures, to produce a purely pentatonic effect:

Idem: 126-127.

b)

The closing theme, in the Mixolydian mode, is again introduced by the woodwind, this time the oboe and flute; and, at its first appearance, it assumes the strophic structure associated with folk song:

17

Idem: 137-146.

a)

At the beginning of the development this theme takes on a *fugato* character:

Idem: 166-170.

b)

114

While later in the same section it appears again as a winding melody (as will be appreciated, each theme has several aspects):

Idem: 186-190.

Next, a kind of trio is inserted; and the development comes to an end with a repetition of the principal theme, now broken up into its smallest sections.

The *reprise* consists only of the pentatonic principal theme; for what, in the exposition, had a merely transitional significance, here assumes the status of principal theme. The function of the coda is a dual one: on the one hand, by recalling the principal theme, it serves as a bridge, rounding off the work as a whole; on the other, by fusing the principal and the closing themes into one, it provides, as it were, a summary of the content.

Seen in its entirety, therefore, *Summer Evening* is in sonata form. But, in the exposition, the development of the different groups of themes plays a larger and more significant part than the usual transitions, and conceals within itself, so to speak, the development of the individual themes. The only exception to this is the closing theme, where the elaboration does actually occur in the development section. Thus, if we consider the beginning of the development section, it appears to be an extension of the exposition; whereas, seen from the end, it has the effect of a *reprise* that has been brought forward.

With regard to the harmonic structure of this work, traces of its classical-romantic heritage are still apparent, yet there are already indications of his most mature and individual style. We have in mind, particularly, his use of chords of the eleventh and thirteenth, and of mixtures, though a number of other characteristic features may also be noted: e. g. the masterly use of counterpoint; the developed sequential technique; and the use of harmonic *glissandos* to produce an effect of suspense.

In the *Dances of Marosszék*, which was written at the same time, the material is largely derived from the collection of Transylvanian folk songs that Kodály had made at an earlier date. Its inception dates from 1923, when he was commissioned to compose a work for the celebrations in honour of the unification of the capital city. At the time, however, knowing that Bartók was also working on a dance suite, he abandoned the idea; and it was not until 1927, that is to say after the *Psalmus Hungaricus*, that it once again began to occupy his thoughts. It was then that he wrote the version for piano, to be followed three years later by the almost identical arrangement for orchestra, the main difference being one of texture; e. g. the semi-tone transposition (in the piano version the basic tonality is C sharp, in the orchestral, D), that is demanded by the fuller sound of the strings.

In form, the work is a short rondo, with three interludes and a coda—the refrain, very characteristically, always returning in a different form. This variation, however, does not so much affect the melody as the formal and harmonic structure of the refrain. The theme of the rondo, with its noble pathos, is an instrumental melodic paraphrase, *rubato* in character, of a Székely folk song of Marosszék in Transylvania—a region where, more than anywhere else, the most ancient kind of dance music has persisted.

18
Dances of Marosszék: 2-25.

The first interlude is a vigorous dance tune, in *tempo giusto* rhythm; the second, a richly ornamented melody in *parlando* style, in which the popular, improvised music of the shepherd's pipe is transformed into art music of the highest quality. This episode, fulfilling the part of the trio and instrumented in the style of chamber music, occupies a central position in the work as a whole. The third interlude suggests another folk instrument, the bagpipe. Above an organ point accompaniment with its mixture of fifths, a throbbing melody in *tempo giusto* races along, almost without ornamentation. The coda also affords new musical material. In a sense it constitutes a fourth episode, straining against the framework of the short rondo; and it very effectively brings the work to a close with a wildly defiant *Hajdú* dance tune.

The principal virtues of the *Dances of Marosszék* are its firm structural outline, the balance that is achieved by the admirable taste with which themes of the most diverse character are associated, the wealth of imagination

116

displayed in the order of the keys, and, despite the homophonic character of the work, its exceptionally varied orchestration. Kodály expressed his own view of its musical significance in a prefatory note: "The Hungarian dances composed by Brahms are typical of urban Hungary around 1860, and were in the main based on the work of composers that were still living. My *Dances of Marosszék* have their roots in a much more remote past, and represent a fairyland that has disappeared."

The other orchestral setting of dance music, composed in 1933, *Dances of Galánta*, also draws upon a vanished past, but a different one. For the *verbunkos* music which inspired it, though also derived from an ancient tradition of folk music, was still flourishing at the end of the 18th century; and though the raw material was, as regards both rhythm and harmony, somewhat monotonous, Kodály succeeded in infusing it with his own creative spirit. Once again it is in rondo form, though here the form is much less strictly observed. After a lengthy *lento* introduction, the majestic principal theme is sounded by the clarinet:

19
Dances of Galánta: 50-58.

With a masterly effect of emphasis, the strophe is repeated, once in full, then again, but this time only the second part of it. Then the sound of the full orchestra dies away, and, after a few bars of *pizzicato*, the first interlude is heard. In contrast to the basic A minor tonality, the sinuous melody played by the flute and piccolo is in the key remotest from it, A flat minor. Then, after a repeat, in which the only variation is in the orchestration, the principal theme breaks out again with passionate intensity. Its single statement, a short thematic transitional passage, links it to the second interlude, which has something of the quality of a song accompanied by the bagpipe. After a repeat, consisting of a fragment of the episode, there is a return of the incomplete rondo theme; and the coda, which comprises more than half of the whole work, opens with a syncopated melody. Such is its wealth of melodic material, that the coda may almost be regarded as a work within a work, its four sections almost constituting an independent formal unity. The last section is built up in a kind of rondo; its principal theme emerges from the soaring, highly ornamented melodies:

20
Idem: 443-450.

Then, for a moment, the gathering impetus is arrested; and the theme of the rondo returns *Andante Maestoso*, in a shortened version, in G sharp minor. After a few bars, however, the subdued, almost timid, tones of the reminiscence are practically overwhelmed by the *Allegro Molto Vivace* confident coda theme, which brings the work to a close with the hammer-blows of four syncopated octave leaps in A minor.

In the harmonic realm there are, thanks to the distinctive character of the music, considerable differences between this work and the *Dances of Marosszék*.

Out of respect for the major-minor melodies of the traditional *verbunkos* music, on which its work is based, functional chord progression is used in preference to pedal points, *ostinato* and mixtures. The type of harmony remains, therefore, more or less within the classical framework, developed, as this had been, by the 19th century masters. It is the style of orchestration that emphasizes the relationship between the two dance rondos. In both cases the composition of the orchestra is almost identical, though in the later work there is more use of percussion and a small part is given to the "Glockenspiel." Similar, too, is the admirable sense of proportion with which pairs of contrasted solo instruments are balanced against the whole orchestra. Where, perhaps, *Dances of Galánta* excels is in its admirable lucidity, in the fuller resonance, and sometimes in the greater brilliance of the orchestra, and in its fascinating instrumental virtuosity.

The two great works that appeared in 1939, the *Concerto* and, to an even greater extent, *The Peacock*, may be regarded as a summation of all Kodály's distinctive gifts as an orchestral composer. Taken as a whole, the *Concerto* is an extremely individual amalgamation of baroque orchestration and form, dance rhythms derived from the Hungarian art music of an earlier period and ancient Hungarian folk melody. Its principal theme, a melody of Kodály's own invention, is purely pentatonic, apart from two "pien" tones that occur on weak beats:

21
Concerto: 1-5.
Allegro risoluto

It is heard first in the strings, then a fifth higher in the woodwind, accompanied by almost the whole of the orchestra. The device of the melody being repeated a fifth higher, and the importance attaching to the interval of the fourth and the fifth, are both specific features of folk music. On the other hand, the strict *tempo giusto* rhythm is characteristic of the popular dance music that was being written at a later date. Certain elements of the theme, especially its fanfare-like opening, can be as readily adapted to polyphonic elaboration as to an *ostinato*. And here, too, just as in *Summer Evening*, we find the inner development already contained within the exposition.

The second subject is an undulating triad mixture on the horns:

22
Idem: 37-39.
Corni

Here, in the internal development, the concerted fanfares of the trumpets are interwoven with certain figures of the theme, somewhat in the manner of an intermezzo; and, after a lengthy thematic transition, in which the principal theme does not occur in the fundamental key, there follows a slow trio. The rhythmically unbroken pentatonic melody, consisting of minims, is also remotely related to the principal theme; and, with the further development of its third bar, the possibilities of imitation inherent in the wide intervals are exploited to the full. The *fugato*, woven in strings and woodwind, intensifies in dynamics and orchestration, and through the retransition, built up from the materials of the principal theme, the quick section enters upon the *reprise*.

119

After a further transitional section, in which motives derived from the principal theme are again made use of, we come to the coda, which begins by echoing the subject of the trio, and then the principal theme from the first movement. Here, the secondary theme is no longer used. Finally, after the utmost possible intensification of the tempo and dynamics of the figures for full orchestra, the work is brought to a close with a vigorous pentatonic figure.

The structure and instrumentation of this work are in *concerto grosso* style, the essential feature of its rapid main section being the sense of movement. In accordance with the theory of J. S. Weissmann, in contrast to the contrapuntal character of this movement the inspiration of the trio, which is of polyphonic construction, is vocal. As one would expect in this form, the whole work is antiphonal, with the solo instruments confronting and responding to larger orchestral groupings. The orchestra, which is one of the largest to be employed by Kodály, consists of four horns, three trumpets, three trombones, a tuba, and percussion; with the addition of a harp in the trio. What particularly distinguishes this work, in addition to its almost baroque dynamism and classical balance, is the exceptionally strict discipline displayed in its construction and the richly varied treatment of the solo instruments.

The other great work of this year, *The Peacock*, is one of Kodály's orchestral masterpieces. Once again, true to his own genius, he draws upon folk music for his inspiration; this time, as we learn from comparative folklore, the most primitive layer of folk music. The theme is a *parlando-rubato*, pentatonic melody, of a descending character with a structure built on interchanging fifths:

23
The Peacock: Original Folk Song.

Bartók described it as "a classic example of incomparable musical concision, from which everything superfluous has been excluded." And it is, indeed, true that in Kodály's style both as a musician and as a writer there is something of the concise, laconic quality inherent in folk song. How, then, is it to be explained that this major work of seven hundred and ten bars is an elaboration of a folk song consisting of only eight bars? The fact is that *The Peacock* is both an expression of Kodály's faith in the inexhaustible creative imagination of the common people and a proof of his own continually renewed melodic in-

120

vention, a work in which almost complete identity between the art of the individual and of the community is achieved. This particular folk song has a special significance for him: he elaborated it for both male choir and mixed choir, as well as taking it for the theme of his greatest orchestral work. Because if its *maqam* character it is inherently in a variation form; and it is in this way that Kodály approaches it, using its elements as the basis not only for his melody and rhythm, but for his scale system and formal structure as well. In the *Peacock Variations* he created a pentatonic melody in double rhythm which is of great originality. And when the folk variant of the theme is heard in the Finale, this is not merely the apotheosis of folk song but also a vindication of the talent displayed by Kodály in the previous variations. In the process of fashioning a song, the people also vary it sometimes; and though such variations may sometimes be the chance result of its having been handed down by oral tradition, sometimes they are conscious and intentional. In the gradual evolution of a folk song, two successive versions may be closely related, and yet there may be little resemblance between the earliest and ultimate versions. And it is in this way that, as a result of innumerable changes, small in themselves, one song eventually grows out of another.

By making use of the almost unlimited resources of art music, Kodály succeeds in developing still further the possibilities inherent in folk song, without in any way losing its essential characteristics. His melodies are based on the pentatonic scale, which readily lends itself to modulation and to line construction, and in which its special character is defined by three fundamental notes. But in this work, though to a lesser extent, Kodály also uses elements that are alien to folk song, such as the tritone, chromatic intervals, whole tones, the Lydian and Locrian modes, and so on. And, indeed, it is precisely this combination of styles that constitutes Kodály's originality.

This great work consists of an Introduction, sixteen Variations and a Finale. Formally, as well as from the point of view of the character of the music, it is divided into three parts: firstly, the Introduction and the first ten Variations; then the next three Variations, forming a sort of trio; and lastly the two remaining Variations and the Finale.

The folk song itself does not appear until the 65th bar, though an outline of it, indicating its pentatonic character, is heard in the bass in the Introduction (and this is further elaborated with five short variations):

24
The Peacock Variations : 2 - 12.
Moderato
Vlc. Cb.

The first change of tonality occurs characteristically when the tritone is introduced (G sharp in the key of D), this being the element most alien to folk song. With the 40th bar there is a burst of passion, that subsides almost immediately.

The First Variation consists of only eight bars. Its instrumental character, and the repeated leaps of fourths, are reminiscent of the principal theme of the *Concerto*. Meanwhile, the outline of the varied figure, a kind of "vocal" development of it, is heard in the trombones. The Second Variation actually consists of two variations: bassoons, violas and 'cellos play a variant rhythmically close to the theme, while a woodwind mixture lingers above them:

25

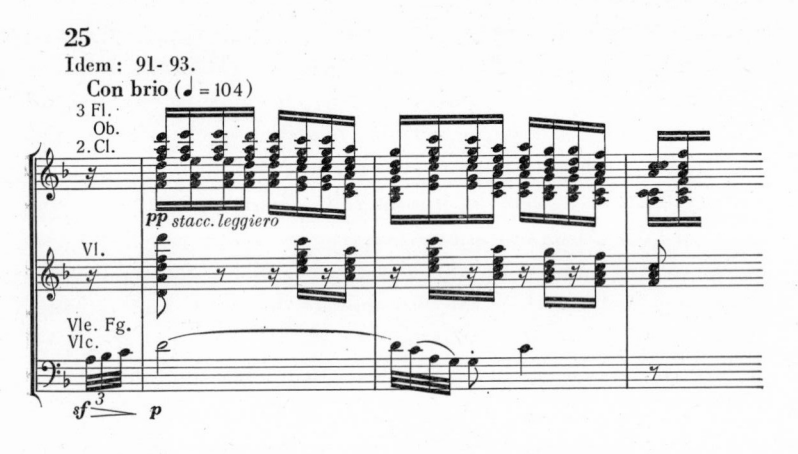

The Third Variation is simpler in structure. Like the First it is of instrumental character, and, since it is in dance rhythm, it is also related to the principal theme of the *Concerto*. The Fourth and Fifth are closely connected twin variations. The former creates a descending minor scale of the theme by further reduction, whereas in the latter the melody is first heard in the base, and then in the upper register, and, in its second section, imitation develops between the outer voices. In the Sixth Variation—of uneven rhythm—the orchestration and dynamics are quieter. While the outer voices proceed in strict canon, the middle voice holds a pedal point on the tonic; then the pedal point descends to the bass, and the melody is heard above it in simplified form with lengthened note values, accompanied by sixth mixtures. In the Seventh Variation there is another change of key, from D minor to the sub-dominant, G minor. Here, the four lines of the theme are condensed into two, whereas in the Eighth, on the contrary, they are expanded internally; the chief characteristic of this variation being the originality of its rhythm, with its playful, dance-like spirit enhanced by the orchestration:

122

26

Idem: 179 - 186.

These eight Variations in *tempo giusto* are now followed by one in *rubato*, in which the melody retains only a remote connexion with the folk-song theme. The accompaniment, too, is completely changed, and consists throughout of light demi-semi-quaver figures on flute and clarinet. In the Tenth Variation, which concludes the first part of the work, the melody is once again condensed into two lines. Its whimsical leaps and peculiar instrumentation—with passages for flute and bassoon in unison, and canons in bare fifths for flute, oboe and bassoon—produce an effect almost of Chinese music, that is a reminder of the Far Eastern origin of Hungarian folk song.

The Eleventh Variation introduces a radical change in every aspect of the work. The atmosphere becomes sombre, with a change of key from D minor to B flat minor. The descending melodic lines, in strophic construction, are replaced by ternary form. At a single stroke we seem to be transported from the Far East to the westernmost part of Europe, though here, too, the occasional pentatonic figures and characteristic leaps of fourths recall the spirit of Hungarian folk song.

With the Twelfth Variation, although the key of D minor returns, the whole atmosphere is made even darker by the use of chromatic mixtures, sustained like an *ostinato* between the extended notes of the melody:

27

Idem: 316-317.

The droning pedal point on the tonic, in bassoons, basses and harp, still further intensifies the fearsome effect, which reaches a tragic climax around bar 330. Even then there is no immediate relaxation. Instead, the music expresses a mood of profound sorrow, bassoons, tympani and lower strings playing a monotonous *ostinato* that suggests the approach of a mourning procession, while the mixtures of the trombones with their insistent rhythm deepen the gloom:

28
Idem: 349-356.

As a result of the chromaticism of the previous Variation, the Thirteenth, which in form resembles the Eleventh, is similarly remote from the spirit of folk song. And these three Variations thus comprise a single group.

The Fourteenth, however, strikes a more optimistic note, its improvisations on the shepherd's pipe producing a mood of cheerfulness. Richly ornamented solos on flute and piccolo are interwoven with runs on the harp and the buzzing of violin tremolos. Finally, in the Fifteenth Variation, the sun shines forth, and the gay $^2/_4$ *tempo giusto* of the melody radiates a spirit of happiness:

29
Idem: 416 - 423.

Then the confident, vigorous dance tune gives way to a free paraphrase, solemn in tempo and pathetic in sound, which leads into the powerful and captivating finale. It is with this appearance of the *tempo giusto* variant of the *Peacock* melody ("The Street of Ürög") that the real apotheosis of the folk song is attained:

124

30

The original folk song on which the finale of the Peacock is based.

The motives of this rhythmical variation are elaborated in a broad style
in the long *Vivace* section with which the Finale opens. In the central section
(Andante Cantabile) the main theme, in a bright major key, sounds triumph-
antly in the strings above triplets in the wind section, so that use is made
of the full sonority of the whole orchestra. The third section *(Allegro)* ful-
fils the role of a coda, in which the lengthened last line of the principal theme,
heard among melodic fragments of the variations, brings the work to a
close on a brilliant note of optimism.

    The structural balance of form and tonality of *The Peacock* ranks it as
a classical work. Its harmonic style is a synthesis, at a high level, of previous
distinctive features, such as the emphasis on mixtures, *ostinato*, and pedal-
point. The harmonic basis throughout the work is functional, with unresolved
dissonances adding new colour to the harmony of the classical composers.
One of the characteristics of *The Peacock* is the way in which each group
of instruments is given a different role, which is sustained consistently
throughout. Another is that both the general line of the voices, and the
detailed development of the figures are derived from the melody, thus giving
the works its completely organic character. With it, not only was Kodály's
place amongst the greatest masters of variation form established beyond
question: he also made genuine Hungarian folk song famous throughout
the world. The development of the ancient melody, with its brilliant orchestral
colouring, does indeed resemble a peacock displaying its magnificent plumage
in the sunlight. Perhaps, of all his works, it gives the fullest expression to
Kodály's love of his fellow men, to his optimism and to his unwavering faith
in the future, based on his confidence in the creative strength of his people.

*

    Finally a few words should be said briefly about the latest addition to
Kodály's symphonic music, the Symphony completed in 1961. This work,
performed for the first time by the Swiss Festival Orchestra on August 16,
1961, at Lucerne, under the direction of Ferenc Fricsay, offers shining proof
of the composer's undiminished creative powers.

The dedication is in itself a symbol: *In memoriam Arturo Toscanini ... Is etenim saepenumero adhortatus est.* It not only pays homage to the source of inspiration, the memory of the great conductor, it not only alludes to their co-operation and to the time that coincides with the origin of the first sketches, but it also points to the unbroken, unswerving line of Kodály's artistic career. The same dedication stands on the fly-leaf of Summer Evening composed in 1906 and revised in 1929-1930.

The key of the composition—C major—its melodic and harmonic world based on pentatony, as well as its treatment of the strings carry a deeper symbolic meaning.

In its entirety the Symphony expresses Kodály's devotedness to a life-work without compromises; it is a confession of faith in the ideals proclaimed for decades — Hungarian folk music and classical traditions. His faithful adherence to these two ideals has spared him the necessity of having to turn back in this late work from the path he had pursued before. Faithfulness to himself is the explanation to why he had no need to embark on a course of experiments in search of new aims, and a clarified pure style.

The unisono introduction of the sonata-form first movement, the principal subject bending into *la* pentatony and unfolding above and below the C organ point, the second subject in A Major and the chords of the closing theme proclaim the unity of the monophonic pentatony of the East and the polyphonic major-minor duality of the West like a programme. The development section is marked by imitation, Kodály's peculiar use of mixtures, and open-work orchestration. The reprise proceeds to the coda in a powerful rise.

The second movement is a type of three-part folk song variation, an apotheosis of the deepest, intrinsic spirit of the folk song. The third movement, flowing attacca from the second, is a finale filled with animated dance rhythms and constructed like a rondo.

This Symphony is retrospection, and at the same time a summation of all the achievements that attained maturity in his earlier chamber music works and symphonic compositions.

Songs and Choral Works

In view of the wealth of orchestral works we have been considering, our contention that Kodály's inspiration is primarily vocal may well come as a surprise. Yet it is scarcely possible to review his work in its entirety without arriving at the conclusion that it is through the medium of singing that he gives expression to his deepest convictions, as well as to his most personal, and artistically most original, spiritual feelings; that it is to the human voice that he entrusts the innermost secrets of his heart.

It was through the writing of songs that his choral style came to maturity; the songs occupying the same place in this respect that his chamber music did in relation to the orchestral works. In this preparatory period, that is to say, prior to the *Psalmus Hungaricus,* he composed nearly fifty songs, including his folk-song arrangements; and only six choral works. But here, too, the *Psalmus* proved to be a turning-point: after it the only independent songs were the *Three Songs* and the nine *Epigrams,* in contrast to some one hundred choral works (though it is true he produced a number of transcriptions, as well as the ten volumes of folk-song arrangements for solo voice, known as *Hungarian Folk Music*). Thus it is clear that, for him, each kind of musical work served as the preparation for another, and that the course of his development was from works for soloists to large ensembles, from orchestral works to vocal music—a fact that throws considerable light on his human, as well as on his artistic, outlook.

As the founder of modern Hungarian art song Kodály understood the nature of his task at an early stage: "It seemed to me," he said in a lecture in 1932, "to be a matter of urgency and importance to develop Hungarian singing, so deeply rooted in the past, so that it might achieve an artistic status comparable to that of singing in other countries. And it was clear that we should only find the way to do this in the musical atmosphere of our villages..." What a succession of poets had laboured for a century to accomplish for literature, he achieved for music by himself and in a single generation: he developed the native musical language of Hungary into a perfect medium for artistic expression. With his songs he solved the fundamental problems of a native singing style. To a considerable extent, his thorough grasp of prosody was the outcome of his activities as scientist and teacher. No other musician had studied the laws of stress and accent of the Hungarian language so profoundly as he; and it was not long before he had established how much they differed from those of Western European languages. As he declared in 1932: "Here we see the tragic results of the fact that, during the last century, our poets made excessive use of the iambic metre. In English, and to a lesser extent in German, French and Italian, iambic rhythms are natural, but they are diametrically opposed to the genius of the Hungarian language. And in consequence many of our literary masterpieces are lost to music. Long ago János Arany pointed out that the iambic and trochaic metres should not be used in Hungarian verse, because such verse when set to music produces songs that are alien to us, unless we distort the rhythm either by forcing the metre or by ignoring it altogether." As early as 1910 he had come to realize that "Greek and Latin metres are more akin to the nature of the Hungarian language, since they are based on groups of syllables more varied and irregular than the iambic and the trochaic. Thus, incredible as it may seem, I was only able to set some of our finest poems to music as a result of what I learned from simple Hungarian songs. It was in a small village, where Berzsenyi's name had never even been heard of, that it first became clear to me how I could set his verse to music..." Another of his discoveries was that, in Hungarian, stress was not a purely dynamic phenomenon, but had a rhythmical, and indeed a melodic, significance as well. And he also found that, when setting verse to music, it was not enough to pay attention only to the word stress, but that the rhythm of the sentence had an even more decisive effect on the shaping of the melody.

If we leave out of account his earliest attempts, Kodály's vocal music may be said to start with *Four Songs*, the first three of which were written in 1907, and the fourth ten years later. Here already the influence of folk song can be felt, mainly in the shaping and treatment of the melody; for the accompaniments show that, in his harmony, he was still a follower of the classical-romantic school. A striking example is the beginning of the second song, *Nausicaa*, which approaches pure pentatony, with the accompaniment adapting itself to it; while the third, *Song of the Field*, even more clearly foreshadows his later work. The final song, *My Heart is Breaking*, was written as part of the incidental music for a play. Its accompaniment (originally for string quintet, cimbalom and clarinet) freed of the excessive ornamentation of the gypsy style of performance, could have served as a model for the composers of popular songs.

*

The sixteen melodies in *Songs* (described as Opus 1) were settings for folk verses that he composed in 1907-1909. The contrasting moods of the different subjects, often condensed into a single line, are given unity by a harmonization rich in ideas. Thanks to the accommodating rhythm and the varying cadences, the declamation of the text is faultless. These short pieces are so akin to the spirit of folk music that one might almost take them for folk-song arrangements. For example, here are the first two lines of the first song:

128

Kodály at Home (Budapest, 1958)

Kodály and "the Musicians of the Future"

31

Though the melody is in fact Kodály's, it sounds like folk music, especially the typical descending pentatonic scale at the end of the second line. Like folk music, too, is the opening statement in a minor key, followed by a perfect fifth on the fifth degree of the scale, which the melody completes, with the characteristic pentatonic suspension 8—7, converted into a dominant seventh by a major triad and followed by a series of dominant sevenths which is also completed by the melody.

Similar elements are also to be found in other pieces in this series which are less closely related to folk song, as, for example, where the third of the tonic triad is replaced by the perfect fourth of the pentatonic chord. On the other hand, as an example of Debussy's continuing influence we may note the entry of a final chord, unrelated to any previous harmony, in the eleventh Song.

Two Songs (Op. 5) is significant, not least of all for the fact that, if we exclude the *Ave Maria* he wrote as a boy, this is Kodály's first setting for solo voice and orchestra. The music of the first song was written to the words of a poem, "The Approaching Winter," by the great writer in classical metre of the 19th century, Dániel Berzsenyi[41]. Here, in conformity with the nature

9

of the text, the atmosphere of the setting is that of art music, rather than folk music. The orchestra has the instrumental melodic character we have seen in his chamber music, the melody beginning with the development of a single motive in sequences. But the middle section of the work already foreshadows the great mixed choruses.

The second of the *Two Songs* is a setting of the poem "To Weep, to Weep," by Endre Ady, the greatest lyrical poet of the 20th century in Hungary. In Kodály, he found a fellow artist fully capable of interpreting, perhaps even of intensifying, through his music the tension and profound sadness of his thought; for the treatment of the text is masterly. The melody is in a sort of free recitative, which, while following closely the subtlest inflections of the verse, at the same time succeeds in conveying the atmosphere of the poem as a whole. The accompaniment—a mixture—moving first in one direction, then oscillating back and forth, is followed by an *ostinato* like the pealing of a bell, that expresses the dark and gloomy colours of the poetry. *To Weep, to Weep* is one of the maturest works of this early period, and is clearly related to the great mixed choruses that were to come later, such as *The Aged* or *Too Late*, and to those parts of the *Psalmus* in comparable mood, like "I only cry and weep..."

By calling the seven songs composed between 1912 and 1916 *Late Melodies*, Kodály implied that the flowering of Hungarian poetry that had begun some one hundred years earlier had not found its musical equivalent. The poems of Ferenc Kölcsey and Mihály Csokonai[42], as well as Berzsenyi, contained material for lovely songs that he was now to set to music. The first of these, *Solitude*, in which the poet is communing with himself, is one of the most beautiful. Instead of the bleak dissonances with which so many contemporary composers were seeking to express the spirit of the early 20th century, Kodály creates a wonderful impression of intimacy by the warmth and brilliance of major triads. A melody in free recitative, once again foreshadowing the melodic style of the later choral works, is heard over a series of chord progressions which are related by the interval of a third, reminiscent of Liszt's later style (*see* musical example on p. 131).

The other outstanding work in this cycle, *Farewell, Carnival!*, is a complete contrast. It displays a clever irony rarely found in Kodály's music. Examples of this are: the impudent, almost arrogant tone of the opening statement; a detailed use of clever imitations; the joking retreat of the carnival, conveyed in syncopated semiquavers; the picture of unctuous, false devotion in the middle section; the ironic use of modal harmonies; and, finally, the explosive outburst of gay carnival spirit in the *reprise*. Of the rest of the songs, some are in the spirit of folk song, some in romantic style; and occasionally he

130

32

Late Melodies (Op. 6): No. 1., 1-11.

The screening shadow of heavenly stillness
Descends upon thee, O sacred Solitude

makes use of those short, *volta* melodies in $^6/_8$ rhythm that recur in the *Psalmus Hungaricus*. The importance of these songs in the development of Kodály's vocal music is due to the perfection with which they express the spirit of these 19th century poets.

The next cycle, *Five Songs* (Op. 9), was composed in 1915 to 1918, and is more or less a continuation of the previous ones, though his individual style is here more marked, especially the very characteristic use of mixtures. All the songs he wrote before 1923 may be regarded as a preparation for the *Psalmus* and the later choruses. Similarly, *Three Songs* (Op. 14), which he wrote between 1924 and 1929, the only cycle to appear after the *Psalmus*, forms as it were an epilogue, or farewell, to the genre. The first of these songs is a setting of a poem by the 16th century lyrical poet, Bálint Balassi; the other two are adaptations of verses by two unknown poets of the 17th century. In both the first and third songs the melody is related very closely to that of the *Psalmus* (in the first, this relationship extends even to the text), though in keeping with their subjective character it recalls the tenor solo rather than the chorus. With the exception of the second song, where it has certain romantic features, the style of harmonization already resembles that of the splendid folk-song arrangements.

As for the nine short pieces, *Epigrams* (1954), originally these had no words, but were written simply as vocal exercises, with piano accompaniment, for use in the class-room. Musically, however, they are considerably above the level of ordinary educational pieces, and, with the texts that have been subsequently adapted to them by Melinda Kistétényi, they are now included in concert programmes. The melodies are a compromise between vocal and instrumental melody; and the original purpose of the songs is clearly revealed by the independence of the singing voice, and the frequent "clashes" resulting from the bold dissonances between it and the upper voice of the accompaniment. The majority of the pieces are harmonized in the classical-romantic manner, without in any way breaking the continuity of style, but the last ones offer a beautiful example of Kodály's harmonic treatment.

*

Before turning to the choruses, a brief reference must be made to Kodály's folk-song arrangements, for it is interesting to examine the principles he followed in his use of folk melodies and the way he developed his harmony and form in accordance with their spirit. The purpose of these arrangements, as Kodály said in the Preface he wrote to the first collection of them that he made jointly with Bartók, was "to enable the general public to get to know and to enjoy folk song... (To this end) we have made a selection of the best of them, and provided them with a musical arrangement that would make them more accessible to public taste. In transferring them from the countryside to the town, some such 'dressing-up,' so to speak, was necessary. But since simply to put them into town clothes would make them awkward and ill at ease, we have tried to design a costume which would enable them to breathe freely. In short, whether we were working for chorus or piano, we have attempted, through the accompaniment, to make up for the fields and villages that are missing."

This, then, was the general principle he worked on: to provide authentic versions of folk songs with conventional accompaniments. While careful to avoid anything alien to the spirit of folk song, he was attempting to make this valuable material attractive to a wide public. To this end, the selection gave preference to those songs in the more recent style, as being closer to urban taste; and he simplified the rich ornamentation of the *rubato* melodies, and so on. When he first started to collect and arrange folk songs, he regarded this ornamentation, which he thought might possibly have been learnt from the gypsies, as inessential to the true folk style of performance. Soon, however, he came to realize that "ornamentation is an organic part of folk singing, and can no more be omitted here than it can from the work of Couperin"— and from then on he gave more and more attention to recording it.

The main body of arrangements, for voice and piano, are the fifty-seven ballads and songs published, between 1924 and 1932, in the series of ten booklets that comprise *Hungarian Folk Music*. In the great majority of these pieces, the accompaniment provided for the solo voice melodies conforms to the vocal part, which it sustains and heightens. The major triad, the dominant seventh chord, as well as the pentatonic (D—F—A—C) and the Wagnerian (B—D—F—A) seventh chords, are prominent; and the harmonization does not extend much beyond these forms with their suspensions. In the basic type of arrangement the accompaniment adds little to the melody and the text; and it is notable that, in the later arrangements, Kodály even decreased the role of the accompaniment. As he came to understand more clearly which notes of the melody were to be supported, he wrote harmonies only under these, though as these basic harmonies are capable of supporting several notes or characteristic melodic figures, the harmony became more varied. With the use of fewer chords, and the grouping together of larger units, the vitality of the songs increased. A classic example of this is Song 55, *Under the Hills of Csitár*, where, with the least possible addition of art music, he brings out the folk spirit of the song most successfully. Some idea of this may be gathered from the first line of the stanza, which is built up on the familiar linear model, AABA:

33
Hungarian Folk Music: No. 55.

Another type of arrangement is one in which the accompaniment adapts itself to the melody, as in No. 47, *My Geese, My Geese*, where the melody is followed by a mixture:

34

Idem: No. 47.

Molto allegro

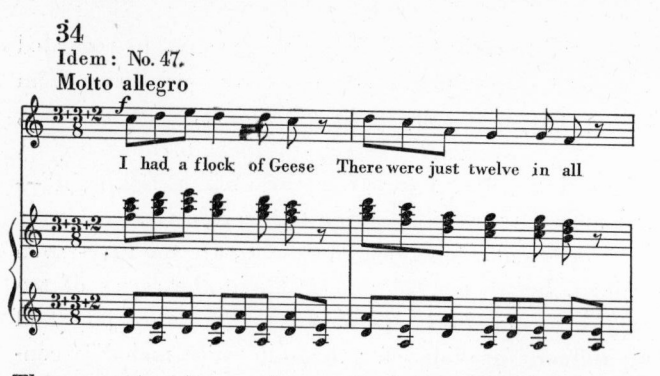

The accompaniment does not always, however, follow the whole melody, as in this case: sometimes it only repeats a figure, or another characteristic feature. In the second stanza of *Little Apples* (No. 5), for example, the piano part is built on the characteristically syncopated rhythm of the third bar:

35

Idem: No. 5.

Con moto

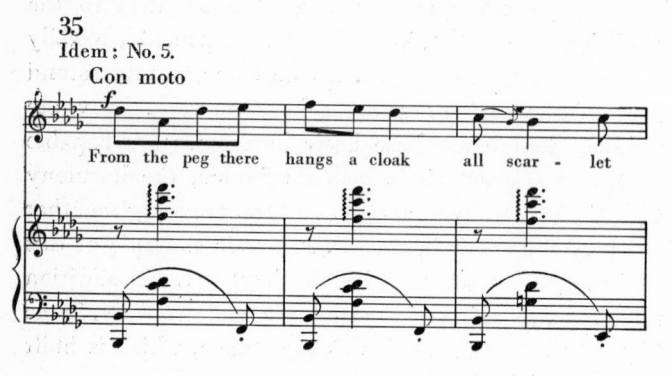

Another variation of this technique may be seen in *All My Days Are Clouded* (No. 38), where the composer has transformed the opening theme of the song into an instrumental ornamentation:

36

Idem: No. 38.

Rubato, quasi adagio

In yet another type of arrangement the accompaniment is derived not simply from the melody itself, but from what the melody and the text have in common. Examples of this may be found in *Wheelcart, Barrow* (No. 12), and *The Sisters* (No. 19), in both of which the *ostinato* type of accompaniment derives from such an inspiration.

In a fourth type of arrangement the accompaniment serves to heighten the dramatic element inherent either in the text as a whole, or in particular stanzas. This is noticeable in the lovely ballad arrangements, such as *Mónár Anna* (No. 1), *The Heartless Wife* (No. 8), *Barcsai* (No. 17), or *Kádár Kata* (No. 18), to mention only the best known. These strengthen the dramatic elements inherent in the text.

An example of the latter is *The Bachelor* (No. 4), which is actually a set of character variations by stanzas, or *A Little Bird* (No. 3), whose madrigalism points ahead to the sections of the great choruses constructed with a similar technique. In this group, the interludes in the accompaniment are especially significant, since they serve both to develop the dramatic situation and to prepare for a change of mood appropriate to the introduction of a new character. Consider, for example, No. 4, where the piano accompaniment interprets the mood of the text with the greatest economy of means. The opening verse, "It's time I was married, It's time to get started," is simply narrative, and this is brought out by the peaceful, ambling style of the accompaniment:

37
Idem : No. 4.

In the following verses four different types of women are introduced. The first is "a young lady, who can neither weave nor spin":

135

The second is old, and "her every word is a storm in heaven":

The third is a "poor beggar girl":

And the fourth is a rich woman, who is continually abusing the other for living at her expense:

Then comes a verse in which the bachelor hesitantly asks: "O what shall I do, then?", followed by the final one in which he suddenly decides to remain a bachelor as he has always been; and the accompaniment expresses the change in his mood with its transition from musing pianissimo to groups of loud, snapping chords.

The examples we have given are perhaps sufficient to illustrate the essential qualities of Kodály's folk-song arrangements: above all his intuitive understanding of the folk spirit of the originals, and his gift for re-interpreting this without in any way distorting it. And this is equally true of the choral folk-song arrangements, though here his richness of invention is even more striking. Moreover, the folk choruses served an additional purpose: by break-ing away from the alien spirit of the "Liedertafel" style, they helped to pre-pare the public for the great independent choral works by Kodály and Bar-tók that were yet to come.

Of even greater significance was the influence these choruses exerted on Kodály's development of form. This is clearly shown in the three large-

136

scale works: *Songs of Karád,* for male-voice choir; *Mátra Pictures,* for mixed choirs; and The *Kálló Folk Dances,* written for a mixed choir and folk orchestra. The *Songs of Karád* is in three- part. In the first, a tavern scene, the three verses of the folk song that are chosen as its basis are heard in varied form. The second is a ballad about a captured outlaw, which consists of two interwoven folk songs, the first depicting his defiant attitude before the court, and the second his cringing entreaties for mercy. The third part is a swineherd's dance, and is written in three-part form, that ends with a coda attached to an unvaried *reprise.* About the whole work, despite the tragic collapse of the outlaw, there is a sense of optimism, the feeling that, whatever may befall, life must still go on.

Mátra Pictures, which comprises three long episodes, is structurally more complex. The first part, which is in rounded three-part form (A—B—A), describes the tragic fate of Vidrócki, the famous outlaw of the Mátra mountains. With the second part, which is not a continuation of the ballad, the atmosphere completely changes; and it is only the joyful exuberance of the finale that establishes the unity of the work as a whole. This last part is in rondo form, with two episodes. The rondo theme, which is divided into five—or more precisely six—voices, is a masterly combination of two folk songs; and the vigorous polyphony of this part is brought to a close with a short coda.

The *Kálló Folk Dances,* once again in three parts, is a simpler work. The soaring, *tempo giusto* dance melody of the first part is heard alternately in the women's and the men's voices. This is followed by a quicker, bagpipe-like movement, and the work concludes with a sweeping finale. The melodies used here were recorded by Kodály in 1938, at Nagykálló, a town in eastern Hungary, where they had obviously persisted for centuries in unchanged form; and the local instrumental style is also preserved in the orchestral accompaniment.

In these works, and in others such as *The Peacock, Székely Lament* and *Mónár Anna,* the structure is mainly homophonic, the melody being sustained by one or two voices, while the other voices serve to accompany the text or give added point or tone-colour. From them, we can realize how organically Kodály's entire musical style is rooted in folk song—not only his use of pentatonic scales, but his melodic and structural invention, as well as his exceptional skill in the use of variation form.

*

Coming now to the children's choruses, we enter a miraculous world, for with these small masterpieces Kodály opened a new chapter in the history of choral music. What above all distinguishes them is the fact that, as Aladár Tóth has said, "the only instrument capable of performing them is the child's voice." Not only do they speak to and about children, but also they may be said to have originated in Kodály's realization, firstly, that in children the creative instinct is inherent, whereas they must be educated to reproductive art and, secondly, that because the child's way of thinking is objective and free of romantic attitudes, real children's music can therefore only be classical music.

Most of the material for these choruses, both text and melody, is drawn from folk song. In those cases where it is not, Kodály selects his texts with great care, the style of the verses set to music is always simple, lucid and concise. The melodies are plastic and easy to sing; and his customary concern for euphony is especially marked here. Wherever possible, he avoids major-minor tonality; and though in the earlier choruses he frequently uses Aeolian, Dorian and Mixolydian scales, in the later ones pentatony is more usual. In general, especially in the choruses inspired by folk song, the rhythm of the melody is closely adapted to that of the text, to which it gives added vitality. Sometimes, however, he introduces a stiff, almost monotonous rhythm, particularly in religious works, such as the very beautiful *Whitsuntide*, where the contrast in the moods of the different movements, strung together in the form of a suite, is heightened even more by the contrasting rhythms. Here, the solemn piety of the first and third movements is counterpoised by the cheerful gaiety of the second and fourth:

38
Whitsuntide: 1-4, 80-83, 179-182, 208-211.

In the second movement, the alto and mezzo voices are a good example of the imitative use of music that is so frequent in these children's choruses, the accompaniment here suggesting the pealing of a bell. Elsewhere, similar devices abound—such as the prolongation of vowel-sounds to imply waiting, or a run of upward-soaring, octave leaps to indicate flight—all of which help to bring out the meaning of the words, as well as making the choruses fun to sing. Often the separate voices are used to personify individuals, the soprano usually representing youth, and the alto age, as in the dialogues that occur in *The Deaf Boatman*, *The Angels and the Shepherds* or *Lengyel László*.

The last of these is a musical version of a favourite children's game, of folk origin, in which Kodály revives a form of polyphony dating from before Palestrina, the so-called "quodlibet" singing, or motet. Two melodies, differing in mood and rhythm, are heard simultaneously: in contrast to the Germans, represented by the altos, who are demanding that a bridge shall be repaired, we hear the sopranos, or Magyars, recalling the glories of times gone by. Out of a simple children's game, Kodály creates a work that brings to life the history of the Hungarian people, and yet miraculously remains genuine children's music:

39

Con moto ♩ = 138

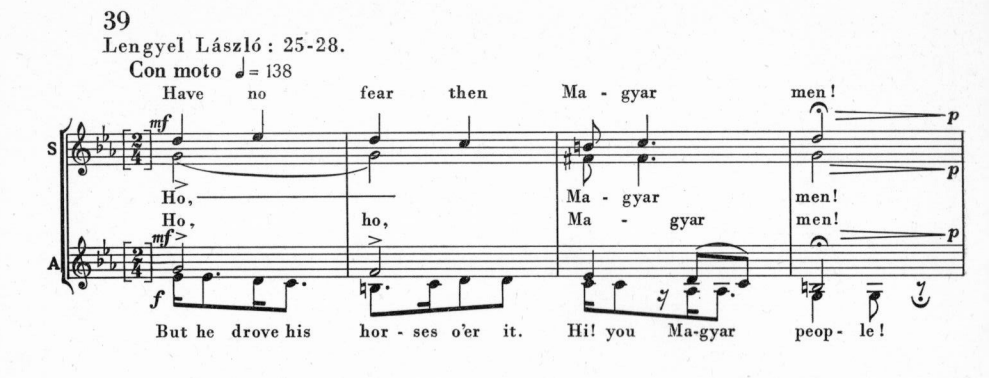

As regards their form, while the earliest choruses are large, complex, cyclical works, the later ones tend to be much shorter, based on a single theme. Characteristic of them all is their strict formal discipline, their lucid structure, and the use of variation form in place of strophic construction. Harmony is not excluded, but more use is made of linear part-writing, in which the voices are increasingly independent; while the unity of the choruses is strengthened by the frequent use of imitation and canon. While displaying the most skilful use of polyphony, these little masterpieces nevertheless retain their essential simplicity. And indeed, in using western polyphony to ornament eastern pentatony, Kodály was creating a system of pentatonic counterpoint—a precious gift to those for whom this music was written, music that displays so abundantly his sympathy with the two great realities of childhood, phantasy and play.

*

For this chapter on the mixed voice choruses we might well take as the epigraph Kodály's own words: "Music that seeks to proclaim the fullness of life demands the fullness of the human voice." For these great works, for which the choruses for men's and women's voices were the preparation, reveal the composer at the height of his powers. The great majority of them were composed in the 'thirties and 'forties; and it is remarkable that the one exception, *Evening*, which dates from 1904, already reveals a number of features common to the later ones. For example, the oscillating movement of mixtures that, right at the start, establishes the basic mood of the work, and is confirmed by the lullaby-like effect at the end; the recitative-like melody, in which each rise and fall of the music is charged with significance; and the use of the lower voices as accompaniment. There is, too, the same method of composition: the upper voice is often the first to introduce the text (with the lower voices subordinated to the highest, despite their musical

140

individuality and polyphonic use), serving as it were to launch the action, while the content is expressed through the polyphonic texture. This may be clearly seen at the opening of *Evening*, where, after a static musical passage that conveys a deep sense of immobility, there follows a moving section depicting the evening star. And there is yet another mark of the maturity of his craftsmanship in this early work—the way in which he seizes upon the possibilities presented by the contrasts inherent in the text. Consider the digression in the tonality and the dynamic contrast in the passage, "Now the noises of earth subside, and heaven's harmony rings forth":

40

Evening : 42-48.

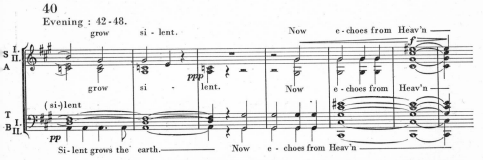

At this climax the music gradually slows down, to produce once again the lullaby effect heard in the opening, and with a subdued major triad the voices bring the work to a peaceful close.

It would appear, then, that right from the beginning Kodály had discovered the key to choral writing. At least it is certain that *Evening* contains more, and more essential, evidence of his mature style than any of his contemporary orchestral works. Yet almost three decades were to elapse before, in 1933, he produced his second mixed chorus, *The Aged;* shortly to be followed, however, by *Jesus and the Traders* and *Too Late.* A notable feature of all these mature works (the same thing is to be found also in *Evening*), is the great static passage with which they open, and which determines the basic atmosphere. At the same time this indicates that in Kodály's personality the epic-lyrical inclination is dominant. As the static passage comes to an end, the dramatic elements also arise, but the start is never *in medias res*, it is rather in the manner of an introductory statement. The introduction to *The Aged* (see musical example on p. 142) is of this type: a rounded exposition creating an essentially uniform impression:*

 * A pitiful sight, these aged folk!
  For sometimes I see them pass by my window,
  their weary backs bent 'neath gathered faggots,
  in wind and in rain, as homeward they go. (Translated by Elisabeth M. Lockwood)

41

The Aged : 1-8.

Here, the forlorn quality of the opening soprano, its contemplative hesitancy gradually giving place to monotonous resignation, sets the tone for the whole picture of sad and aging people. And similarly in *The Norwegian Girls*, the mood of the whole poem is firmly established by the first few bars:

42

Norwegian Girls : 1-6.

In this case, the double pedal point of the alto voice creates an impression of heavy mist, with the care-free girls of Balholm (sopranos and tenor) strolling along the quay-side. This is the static passage that establishes the tone of the whole work, and which the strophic construction later elaborates.

142

Two further examples of a similar use of this introductory statement are the four voices singing in unison at the beginning of the *Ode to Franz Liszt:*

43
Ode to Franz Liszt: 1-2.
Maestoso, ma con moto

Fore - most 'mid the world's great mu - sic mak - ers,

The pentatonic symbol at the beginning of the work pledges faith in the Hungarian spirit of Franz Liszt.

The introduction of the *Dirge* has a similar significance. Here the salutation is to the "mute companions," to the dead comrades.*

44
Dirge : 1-16.
Maestoso

Óh, ti né - ma tár - sak, bús, ha-lott ba - rá - tok, Le-sza-kadt re -

Óh ti né - ma tár - sak, bús, ha-lott ba - rá - tok

á - tok a nagy vé - res á - tok. Vit - té - tek a tü-zet, a

Le - sza-kadt re - á - tok a nagy vé - res á - tok. Vit - té - tek a

meny-nye - i szé - pet, Míg az ő - rült rém jött, s min-dent ösz - sze - té - pett.

meny-nye - i szé - pet, Míg az ő - rült rém jött, s min-dent ösz - sze - té - pett.

* O you mute companions, sorrowful, dead comrades,
The great curse of blood is upon you.
You had borne the fire, the celestial, beautiful fire
Till the raving Spectre came and destroyed all.

In another group of the mixed choruses—e. g. *Psalmus Hungaricus, Zrínyi's Appeal, Jesus and the Traders,* and *To the Magyars*—Kodály makes use of a testo-type introduction: an affirmation, as it were, to which the ensuing drama serves as a commentary. In the *Psalmus,* where it is the chorus that makes the affirmation, it reminds us of the contemplative choral sections in Bach's *Passions,* representing an objective commentary by the community, that are interspersed amongst the lyrical arias. But in *Zrínyi's Appeal* the position is reversed, the chorus personifying, not the contemplative crowd, but the agitated individual, who breaks into the narrative of the verse-chronicler, jerking us back into the evoked present. The prose work from which Kodály took the story—*Medicine Against the Poison of the Turk,* by the 17th century patriotic poet and military leader, Miklós Zrinyi—opens with the words, "At the taking of the town of Sardis, a warrior, coming into the presence of King Croesus himself, sought to slay him." So, here these opening words are given to the solo baritone:

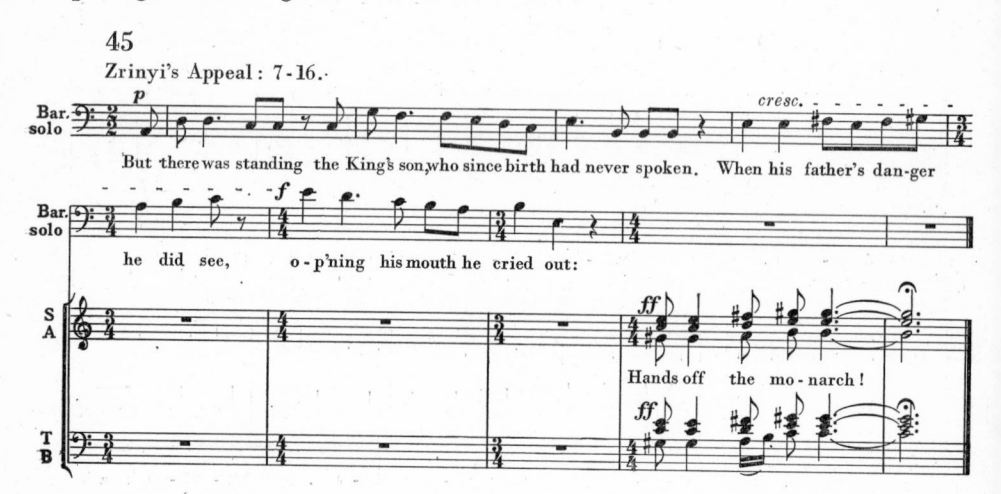

45

Zrinyi's Appeal : 7-16.

In its dramatic effect—and even in the words—the intensified sound of the chorus, coming in at this point, reminds us of the double chorus in the *Saint Matthew Passion, So ist mein Jesus nun gefangen,* where the second chorus breaks into the first with insistent, dramatic comments, *Läßt ihn, bindet nicht.*

What all the examples so far cited have in common is that the structure is determined, not primarily on musical grounds, but rather by the logic of the text and the dramatic demands of the story. A further common feature of the choruses is that Kodály strengthens or renders permanently valid the credence of the subjective message, its sincere truth, with a "more objec-

Kodály with Yehudi Menuhin

Kodály at Oxford University, after Receiving the Honorary
Degree of Doctor of Music

tive" element. And when we come to examine the structure of the choruses, we find a classical balance between the homophonic and polyphonic passages. The use of linear construction serves a dual purpose: it expresses perfectly the spiritual atmosphere he requires, and makes each part easily singable. The aims of composition and performance are not at variance with each other, indeed, united they strengthen the homogeneity of the work. Similarly, the vertical mode of thought ensures a perfect blending of the voices that produces a compact quality in the choruses, and so in turn helps to make the works easy to sing. Since the choice between homophonic and polyphonic forms is largely determined by the text, none of the choruses is solely either one or the other. Sometimes both forms are used consecutively, thus affecting the structure of the work; and sometimes simultaneously, affecting the texture of the voices. When used consecutively, a polyphonic section is often inserted between two homophonic sections, or sometimes the two forms are used alternatively, in accordance with the requirements of the text. For a narrative or lyrical mood homophony is more often used, but for dramatic movement polyphony; whereas, when emphatic statement is demanded by the text, voices are used in unison. Where the ancient technique of double imitation is used, through the imitation of two pairs of voices at a time, the construction is simultaneously homophonic and polyphonic as in the passage from *Dirge*, already quoted (*see* 44th musical illustration, p. 142).

In these choruses, in order to bring out the full significance of the text, Kodály draws upon all the resources of melody, rhythm, accent, dynamics and harmony. Most comprehensive is the characteristic way in which he makes use of harmony as an element of construction—blocks of chords and mixtures serving as the basis for considerable musical units, and even for entire works. For shorter passages, however, he relies rather on melody and rhythm, which he adapts to the text, not in the *parlando* style of folk song, but with a full realization of the potentialities of art music and, at the same time, with the most consistent attention to prosody. Indeed, his admirable understanding of prosody is one of Kodály's greatest assets as a vocal composer; an understanding based partly on his instinctive feeling for the language, and partly also on careful observation and the study of phonetics which he had undertaken at the university. But his mastery in adapting words and music is not solely dependent on his knowledge of prosody: he also exploits possibilities that are afforded only by music. For example, whereas words can only be spoken consecutively, it is possible to superimpose the corresponding musical sounds, and, as we have seen, Kodály makes use of this device both for heightening the mood and shaping the structure of the music. Or, again, he sometimes intensifies the sense of the text by bringing out unspoken

meanings, or illuminating hidden connections, by purely musical means.
A good example of this occurs in the introduction to *Jesus and the Traders*:
"As the feast approached then Jesus went up and enter'd Jerusalem."
In the fourth bar the full chorus breaks into the subdued unison passage of
the narrative statement to supply a lyrical comment, expressing respect for
Jesus's courage, and consternation at the presence of his enemies in the temple:

46

Jesus and the Traders : 1-7.

As the feast ap-proached then Je-sus went up and en-ter'd Je-rusa- lem into the Temple

Later in the same work there is a further instance of the meaning of the
text being emphasized by the music, though in this case the effect is also
partly psychological. After the intensely personal setting of the words, "Is
it not written, My house shall be called a house of prayer for all the nations?"
the music divides into two parts: while the bass continues the quotation,
"What have ye made it? A den of robbers," the rest of the voices repeat the
word "Robbers," bringing out the full force of the accusation:

47

Idem : 146-151.

After this outburst the *testo* again proceeds in unison, with the rest of the
voices continually breaking in to express their dramatic reflection on the
story with the single word "Robbers." And here Kodály reveals his remarkable
psychological ingenuity by the way in which the word is interpolated in the
interchanging voices of the text:

48
Idem: 159 - 167.

"When the scribes and the chief priests and... (Robbers)... heard Him... (Robbers)... and sought how they might destroy him... (Robbers)... for they
feared him..." But at this point in the story, "...for all the multitude was
astonished at his teaching," though from the musical point of view it would be
perfectly logical to repeat the cry of "Robbers" yet again, he does not do
so, for here the music follows higher spiritual motives. The interpolated cries
of "Robbers" imply moral condemnation of the scribes and chief priests:
their cessation shows that this condemnation does not extend to the multi-

tude, who feel sympathy for Jesus. Thus he foregoes an effective musical ending in order to achieve a conclusion more in keeping with the spirit of the text.

Kodály also has a variety of ways of bringing out the verbal meaning by musical symbolism, as, for instance, in the chorus he wrote to the beautiful poem by Ady, *Too Late*. As the sopranos sing, "We always, everywhere come too late. Ah, too late," the accompaniment trudges wearily along in a series of slow minims and semi-breves. And the very idea of lateness is epitomized in the conclusion:

49
Too Late: Closing Bars.

Here, the suspensions gradually become consonant to the major triad, the tempo is slowly drawn out, the note values become longer, and the melody almost comes to a halt on the two semi-breves, while the soprano entry is still further delayed. Or, again, consider the passage at the end of *The Norwegian Girls*, where he obtains an impressive effect of atmosphere by the combination of double pedal points, symbolizing the heavy mist, with repeated quavers to suggest the falling rain:

50
Norwegian Girls : Closing Bars.

148

These are a few examples of the superb craftsmanship with which Kodály succeeded in giving expression to his creative imagination in the great mixed choruses, works that not only led to a revival of choral music in Hungary but also occupy a significant place in the long tradition of European choral writing.

Music for the Stage

Properly to evaluate *Háry János* and the *Spinning-Room*, it is necessary to have some idea of the development of opera in Hungary. It was not until the middle of the 19th century, after a number of primitive attemps, that Ferenc Erkel (1810-1893)—the contemporary of Glinka, Moniuszko and Smetana—succeeded in establishing a national Hungarian opera with his two works, *Hunyadi László* and *Bánk Bán*, which at once took their place in the European repertoire. Kodály said of him on one occasion that he "chose the path that made it possible to bring music closer to the people, and the people closer to music. In composing the music for a whole series of folk plays he used genuine folk music. It is a pity that he did not go further, but the gap between folk song and opera seemed to him too big to make any decisive attempt at bridging it. Yet until this has been done, there can be no hope of establishing real contact between the ordinary people and the higher forms of music."

Like the other national operas of the period, Erkel's operas were an off-shoot of the national liberation movement, for though their themes were taken from the history of past struggles, they were addressed to their contemporaries, the builders of the future. After him, development was to take two directions. On the one hand, a product of the romantic democratic movement, there was an outburst of "folk plays"—stylized period pieces, with idealized characters drawn from folklore: on the other, a growing submission in all fields of art music to the pervasive influence of Wagnerism. Neither of these developments was conducive to the further growth of Hungarian opera: the first, because it increasingly tended to supplant the genuine tradition of folk music with the cult of popular art songs, the so-called *Magyar nóta;* the second, because, as Kodály noted, instead of bringing the majority of the people into closer contact with opera, it served only to alienate them from it still further.

Eventually the second influence proved to be the stronger, with the result that, by the turn of the century, there was a strong bias in favour of international, as opposed to Hungarian, music in all departments, including that of opera. This is the fundamental reason why *Prince Bluebeard's Castle*—when, after waiting for seven years, it was finally produced on the stage—failed to achieve success. As Kodály put it: "It was not simply the public who failed to respond: the very walls of the theatre failed to resound to it. It became clear that, before we could hope to win the people for work inspired by their own voice, we must first arouse in them the consciousness of their own musical language, otherwise nothing we might say in that language could be understood by them. This was the task I set myself when writing *Háry János* and the *Spinning-Room*." To this end, the aim he set himself in these two works was the limited one of introducing to the stage original Hungarian folk song. To quote him again: "Once the walls of our theatres and the ears of our people have become attuned to folk music, it will be possible to move on to work of a higher order, music that is less closely earthbound—for then there will be no danger of its being uprooted."

The first of these works, *Háry János*, was composed in 1925-26, that is to say, after the *Psalmus Hungaricus* and contemporaneously with the first issues of *Hungarian Folk Music*. At that time Kodály had little stage experience to draw upon, having hitherto only composed incidental music—for Zsigmond Móricz's play, *Lark Song*, and the first, shorter, version of the *Spinning-Room* in 1924, amongst others. If there is little evidence of experimentation or timidity in his new work, it is because, though still a stranger in the world of the theatre, he was nevertheless thoroughly at home with his characters. The hero, Háry János, was an historical figure, a veteran of the Napoleonic wars who, at the beginning of the 19th century, was living in a small village in Transdanubia. János Garay, who described his exploits in an admirable narrative poem, had known him personally. Kodály introduces him in his Preface as follows: "Háry is a peasant, a veteran soldier, who day after day sits in the tavern, spinning yarns about his heroic exploits and being a real peasant, the stories produced by his fantastic imagination are an inextricable mixture of realism and naivety, of comic humour and pathos. Yet he is by no means just a Hungarian Munchausen. Though superficially he appears to be merely a braggart, essentially he is a natural visionary and poet. That his stories are not true is irrelevant, for they are the fruit of a lively imagination, seeking to create, for himself and for others, a beautiful dream world."

These adventures provide the theme of the play: the emperor's daughter falls in love with him, he defeats Napoleon single-handed, restores order in the Vienna Burg, and finally brings his sweetheart back to his native village. The work is, indeed, an epic, celebrating the strength of the Magyar people, their gallantry and their love for their fatherland. "Behind the mask of lies, exaggeration and phantasy one glimpses, as the essence of the play, the tragedy of the Hungarian dream," Bence Szabolcsi has said. "But it is Kodály's music, not the action or the words, that strikes the note of tragedy."

This music speaks sometimes in the tones of the folk songs—when it depicts real life, or characterizes the Hungarian heroes—at other times it is descriptive, when it tells of adventures in foreign lands. The music of the prologue and of the epilogue builds a bridge between the dream and reality.

The variety of the music offers the widest possible scope to Kodály's ranging imagination, which responds especially to the lyrical warmth and irresistible, mocking humour that are important elements in the play. Of the songs and choruses—and *Háry János* contains exquisite examples of his choral writing—little need be said, for we have already discussed their main stylistic features in previous chapters. The folk songs, which are orchestrated sometimes exuberantly, sometimes with a noble simplicity, have been carefully selected, both for the ensembles and for the solo numbers, to represent the characters and the plot. Thus, just as not a single ancient Hungarian motif is given to the courtiers, so too no melody of alien origin is sung by the Magyar heroes. There is a sharp dividing-line between such music as the lilting minuet of the emperor's daughter, the double chorus of the court ladies preparing for the feast, and the alphabet song of the little princes, on the one hand, and the numerous songs of Háry, his sweetheart, Örzse, and the old coachman, Uncle Marci, on the other. And the latter group contains not only the lyrical climax of the work, the noble duet, *This Side the Tisza, Beyond the Danube*, but also its dramatic climax, the song in which Háry expresses the idea underlying the whole play, *I'll Plough up the Emperor's Courtyard*.

The orchestral music has a unity of its own; and, indeed, a concert version of it, *The Háry János Suite*, consisting of six selections with certain changes of sequence, was subsequently prepared by the composer, as well as an independent version of the *Overture*. In the latter, instead of polyphonic construction, Kodály uses contrasting blocks of chords, a technique which is more in keeping with the character of the music and with the requirements of the theatre. Apart from this, he made few concessions to the theatre, either as regards the length or subject matter of the work. The *Overture* is not so much an introduction to the action of the play, as a summary of its content. Its atmosphere is pathetic, reflecting both the hero's attitude to life and the underlying idea of the play, the contradiction between his bright, heroic dreams and sober reality. The principal theme has a synthetic character: on the one hand, with its dotted notes and syncopated figures, recalling the age-old past to which Háry belongs; and, on the other, using

151

an essentially pentatonic structure and suggestions of folk song to project him as the eternal symbol of his people:

51
Theatre Overture: Principal Theme

After a repetition by sequence one degree higher, in a manner already familiar, the principal theme is then followed, after a short transitional section, by the second subject. Both the transitional section and the second subject are augmented variants of the principal theme, modified by accidentals; and their quality of mystery, their tonal uncertainty, are suggestive of the world of dreams. Here, too, an important part is played by the frequent leaps of fourths and fifths, and by the triad-mixtures of the accompaniment, both of which are so characteristic of Kodály's style.

The third group of themes, inspired by the *verbunkos* music, once again evokes Háry's historical background. Of particular interest is the following variant, with its taut rhythm and measured solemnity:

52
Idem: 186-189.

Naturally, the *Háry János Suite* itself is much more closely connected with the plot of the play than the *Overture*: and, as will be seen, whereas the purpose of the First, Third and Fifth Movements is to convey the background atmosphere of the whole work, the Second, Fourth and Sixth are dramatic evocations of humorous and incredible incidents in the story. The tension between these two groups is emphasized by the contrast between the thematic and instrumental treatment.

The First Movement, *The Tale Begins*, introduces us to the world of Háry's fantastic imagination, while at the same time implying by its passionate tone that underlying it there is a more profound reality. After the quick orchestral figurations and piano *glissando* (representing the sneezing of the incredulous scholar in the story), comes the subdued five-bar motive on the 'cellos and basses, from which the whole movement is built up. This short piece has a uniform atmosphere and the theme is freely developed to reach a double climax: after a sudden passionate outburst, the mood grows calmer and the movement closes on a note of peacefulness.

152

For the Second Movement, *The Chimes of Vienna*, the orchestra is completely transformed: the strings and bass instruments being replaced, in keeping
with the theme, by the high- and medium-range wind instruments, percussion, carillon, bells, celesta and piano. The principal theme is a melody based
on triads with a lively rhythm, and is in the rondo form used by Couperin,
admirably suited to the woodwind:

53
Háry János Suite: II, 5-8.
  Allegretto

After each of the three episodes the rondo theme returns, with the melody
unchanged but different orchestration. The irresistible humor of the Movement is emphasized by its exaggerated regularity: its eight-bar principal
theme with its regular periods, episodes of identical length, small units
responding to each other, and the rigidly precise alternation of the ensemble.

In sharp contrast to this, the next Movement, telling of Háry's love
for Örzse, is filled with the tenderest emotion. Here Kodály chose as the
theme the loveliest of the folk songs from his Opera, *This Side the Tisza,
Beyond the Danube*. Again, the constitution of the orchestra is changed: in
addition to the high woodwind and the horns, the cimbalom is introduced
and the strings are brought back. The twelve-bar theme is heard for the first
time in the violas, and in the *reprise*, though the melody is unchanged, there
are variations of the accompaniment. This is a short Movement, that soars
upwards in a single passionate curve, before subsiding and dying away.

The Fourth Movement, *Battle and Defeat of Napoleon*—in which, of
course, Háry defeats the whole army single-handed—is in three parts, the
first of which, the procession, opens with a bouncing theme on the trombones
and trumpets:

54
Idem: IV, 5-12.
  Trbni.

The humorous atmosphere here is heightened almost to the point of ludicrous-
ness by the use of an accented augmented fourth at the end, and by the major

153

seventh used later in the trumpet calls. A long trill leads to the second part, the battle scene, in which a climax of grotesque effect is reached in a passage for three piccolos, two trumpets and two trombones, with the harsh tones of the trombones emphasizing the effect. The "heroic" aspect of the battle is caricatured in the opening *glissandos* on trombone and bass tuba. The third part, *Napoleon's Lament*, is accompanied throughout by subdued *glissandos*. The mock-melancholy theme, the hiccoughing *appoggiaturas* and nasal tone of the saxophone evoke laughter, while the brevity of the three parts intensifies the humorous quality of the whole movement. The effect is heightened by the lavish orchestration and the use of alien melodic phrases attached to the basically pentatonic framework.

In the Fifth Movement, the *Intermezzo*, this spirit of mockery completely disappears, and in its place we have a noble vision of Hungary's greatness, the essential idea at the heart of the whole opera. It is in song form, with a trio; the material, both in the main section (which is in three-part form), and in the trio (in two-part form), is derived from the literature of the 18th and 19th century *verbunkos*. Here it is not simply a matter of arrangement: so closely has Kodály identified himself with the spirit of the period that he succeeds in actually recreating the style of one of the most characteristic types of Hungarian dance music. He decorates the featureless melodic outline with vigorous rhythms, preserving the essential spirit of the dance while providing it with the most original harmonization.

With the final Movement, *Entry of the Emperor and his Court*, the spirit of mockery and caricature returns, sustained once again by the large-scale instrumentation and the brevity of the melodies, and by the humorous contradiction between the alien melodic phrases and the essentially pentatonic structure. In Háry's imagination the high dignitaries of the court become fairy-tale figures, and their ceremonious entrance is reduced to farcical capering in the accompaniment to the two themes reproduced below:

55
Idem: VI, 5-12.
Alla Marcia

56
Idem: VI, 17-20.

Here, as in the Second and Fourth Movements, Kodály is in no way concerned to create a realistic representation of the world of courts and statesmen. What he does do, with consummate artistry, is to reveal the effect produced by these "heroes" in the mind and imagination of an ordinary peasant. Out of these six pieces, with their sharp contrast of mood and treatment, what emerges is a convincing portrayal of Háry, the typical representative of the whole Hungarian peasantry. When he is writing of the great world to which the peasants are strangers Kodály adopts a mocking, critical tone. But when they, the ordinary people, are his subject, his confidence in their future touches his music with sublimity.

In his other stage work, the one-act Spinning-Room, it is once again the Hungarian people who are the heroes. In its seven scenes he brings together twenty-seven songs, ballads, dances and musical games, selected from the rich harvest that he had himself, at one time and another, gathered from the lips of the peasants—even the dramatic narrative that serves to link these pieces together is drawn from folk song. Obviously, a work constructed in this way can in no sense be described as an opera. But though the Spinning-Room is not an opera, it is by no means easy to decide what musical category it does belong to. Perhaps it may best be described as a dramatic rhapsody, or an operatic folk ballad; and certainly what gives it its unity is the unchanging, yet constantly evolving, spirit of folk song. In so far as it can be said to have a plot, it is the story of two lovers, who, after many adversities, are happily reunited. But between their sorrowful parting and happy reunion the vivid music of orchestra and chorus portrays all the joy and suffering and optimism of life in a typical Székely village.

The Spinning-Room is built up almost entirely from the various choral items, and affords an admirable opportunity for Kodály to display the beauty of the "Hungarian counterpoint" he had invented. Typical of the ensembles are the part-writing in imitation, the simultaneous sounding of two different folk songs, and the many other musical devices that we have considered previously. The orchestra is given no independent role, but is used throughout only for accompaniment, save on two occasions: the short, suggestive introduction in unison, and the passionate intermezzo of seventy-two bars. Of the twenty-seven vocal settings the best known are Cockricoo, Görög Ilona, Under the Hills of Csitár, The Bachelor and The Heartless Wife; but all of them are admirable examples of Kodály's superb gift for arranging folk song. A number of them had already appeared before (in issues of Hungarian Folk Music) the production of the Spinning-Room, with simple piano accompaniment; and some critics now expressed the view that the melodies were more effective in this version than in the more elaborate operatic arrangement. To this criticism, however, Kodály himself replied conclusively: "It was precisely through hearing these songs in the concert hall," he wrote, "that I realized that, torn from their natural environment, they are scarcely intelligible. The whole purpose of my present experiment was to attempt to display them in a living unity with the life from which they have sprung... The *Spinning-Room* is not an experiment in opera, because I wanted to be certain of my ability to achieve the task I had set myself. Some critics have even objected because the songs are linked together by simple speech, and that I have made no use of *recitativo*. But this is to miss the point: the use of *recitativo* would have been a violation of the style of the work."

Thus, though both *Háry János* and the *Spinning-Room* have been produced on a number of occasions in many European cities, there can be no question of Kodály having established a Hungarian national opera worthy of taking its place in the operatic repertoire of the world. One prerequisite for this is the emergence of a tradition of national drama, but in this field the standard of Hungarian writers is below that of their other work; and the same may be said of our composers. Certainly, in these two masterpieces, Kodály's music has a dramatic quality, but what first captivates the listener is their narrative strength and lyrical beauty. Yet if the creation of contemporary Hungarian opera remains a task for the new generation, at least it will always be recognized what a masterly contribution to it was made by Kodály.

Choral Works with Orchestra

If the mixed choruses proclaim "the fullness of life... with the fullness of the human voice," in the *Psalmus Hungaricus*, the *Te Deum of Budavár* and the *Missa Brevis* Kodály may be said to have declared his belief in the ultimate unity of life and art. These three great oratorial works, written for symphony orchestra and organ, with solo voices and full chorus, are his crowning achievement.

The *Psalmus Hungaricus*, which he composed in little more than two months, marks the end of the two years of silence that separated the period of the songs and chamber music from that of the choruses and orchestral works. In the first of these periods he had, as we have already seen, achieved a technical mastery of vocal and instrumental style. Here he displays an astonishing maturity in the way he succeeds in fusing these styles; and, what is even more astonishing, in this his first work for a large ensemble, he already shows himself to be at the height of his powers.

156

It is significant that he chose for his theme a poem that spans the history of civilization, the fifty-fifth psalm. First sung by King David some thousand years B. C., then freely adapted by the Hungarian poet, Mihály Kecske-méti Vég, during the period of the Turkish occupation of his country, Kodály was to give it a new lease of life in the 20th century. Always it had been the song of the persecuted and afflicted, at once the expression of their sorrow and bitterness and the source of comfort and hope for the future. And if, now, Kodály was able to express through his music the passionate feeling of the poem, it was because all the humiliations of the past years were still alive in his memory.

If the text may be regarded as a synthesis of past and present experience, so too may the music. For pentatonic phrases are discernible even in the diatonic and chromatic sections, blending in the most natural way with harmonies and forms of western derivation.

The work opens with a short, passionate orchestral introduction. The sorrowful cries of the instruments subside to a dull rumble of tympani, and the voice of the chorus is heard, in its role of commentator, opening the drama with its unison chant:

57
Psalmus Hungaricus: 16-24.
Tranquillo

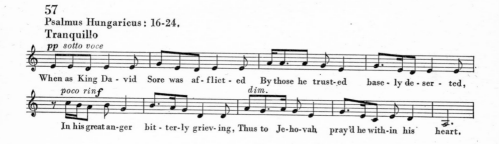

This melody, pentatonic in character, is in the rhythm of a Galliard, and is the principal theme of the work, which is in rondo form. It returns five time as a chorus *ritornello*, continually giving strength to the basic mood of the poem. It is interesting that Kodály here treats the introductory or-chestral material in an unusual way, one might almost say as a second rondo theme. Its ro   identical with that of the principal theme, although it does not return so often, and its position is less symmetrical, so that it always preserves its introductory character. It introduces the chorus *ritornello*, and, immediately after the chorus, it introduces the first episode; later it precedes the second section of the work, the Entreaty (the fourth episode), and finally the Epilogue (the last chorus *ritornello*). Thus the structure of the *Psalmus* is built up on a firm dual basis of vocal and instrumental themes.

157

In the episodes the tenor solo is dominant, it leaves only the last of the six to the chorus and joins with it in the fourth. The plaintive voice of the psalmist is heard over the tremolos and trills of the strings:

The mood of the second verse is one of increasing bitterness, the lamenting tones of the solo being accompanied by the solemn and mournful harmonies of the strings:

Then, in his desolate loneliness, the poet begins to think of the possibility of escape, and in the third verse this is expressed by the greater resolution of the music. This is followed by the chorus *ritornello*, which, though still in unison, has a different character: it is heard above the wailing accompaniment of the orchestra, a fifth higher and forte. And here it is no longer heard as an objective affirmation but as the voice of the actively participating multitude.

In the three verses of the second episode the poet once again pours out the sadness that is in his heart, his tone becoming increasingly passionate as he enumerates the perfidious deeds of his enemies. The accompaniment, too, grows more agitated, the semi-quaver runs flashing with anger. The melody rises a major second, and the fortissimo sound of the eight voices of the mixed chorus, here reinforced by a children's choir, indicates that it is no longer a

158

question of a crowd of onlookers, but of an active community, welded into one by their common grief and expressing their sympathy and readiness to help.

With the growing intensity of the third episode, we approach the climax of the first part of the work, the poet's lament as he speaks of the hardest blow of all: "For it was not an enemy that reproached me... But it was thou... my companion and my familiar friend." Here, the soloist begins piano, then rises to forte; and as his voice ceases, the orchestra takes over his lament with a great fortissimo. There is a moment of silence. Then the tension is broken by the Old Testament curse: "Let death come suddenly upon them, Let them go down alive into the pit":

60
Idem : 178
Tenor solo
ff marcatissimo

Smite them with de-struc-tion —

Here, it would be almost impossible to overstress the exclamatory quality of the music. The solo voice enters *ff marcatissimo*, in a passionate outburst without any accompaniment. At first it seems that the instruments have been shocked into silence, but when later they come in with a series of excited runs and *tremolos*, the effect is intensely moving. The dramatic quality of the interlude is increased by the way in which Kodály here compresses what he has to say into two stanzas, instead of the previous three. And this effect of compression is reinforced by the third and fourth interludes being separated, not by the chorus *ritornello*, but only by the shorter orchestral rondo theme; and the effect is still further heightened by the wordless melody, sung by the chorus, that introduces the second section, the Entreaty. This is the only occasion in the work when solo and chorus unite, in supplication to God. Here, material from the first interlude is used again, but this time, through the technique of imitation by the chorus, what was before the sorrowful complaint of an individual becomes a cry of hope from a community confident of its strength. The chorus repeats the Entreaty, a fourth higher and fortissimo; then, after a pause of one bar, the fifth episode begins. This time even the shorter *ritornello* is omitted, since formal principles must give place, if necessary, to the content and dramatic structure of the music. For the moment Kodály offers no explanation for this. But what follows is even more unexpected. We hear soft *arpeggios* on the harp, coloured by *pizzicato* notes and harmonies on the strings and *pp* chords on the flutes; and the key to this sudden, ethereal vision in the midst of the lamentation is given by the tenor solo, as he sings, "Cast thy burden upon the Lord, and he shall sustain thee: He shall never suffer the righteous to be moved":

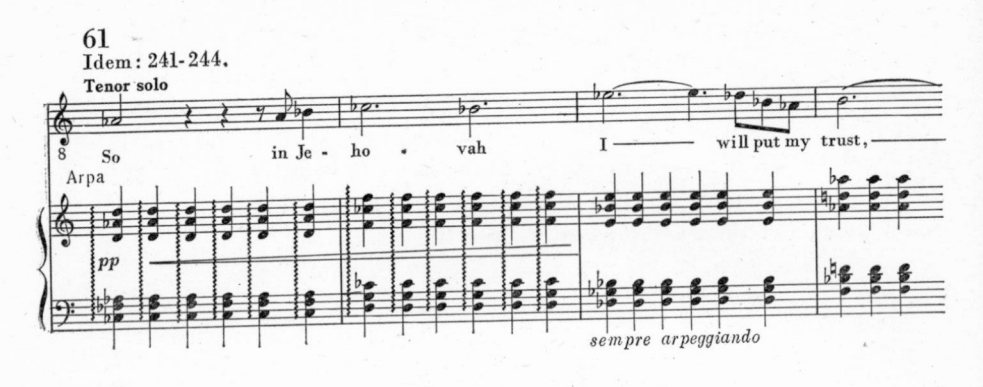

61
Idem : 241- 244.

With this the poet bids farewell: having accomplished his mission of uniting his people, his soul has found comfort. Then we hear the chorus, singing the people's hopeful confidence and praising the stern God, who exalts the poor, but "brings down into the pit of destruction... bloodthirsty and deceitful men." This section, with its use of imitation and rich symbolism, is one of the most sublime choral passages in the whole work. The orchestral rondo theme is skilfully woven into the penultimate chorus *ritornello*, the key of which is here changed; and we come to the majestic splendour of the climax, to the second part:

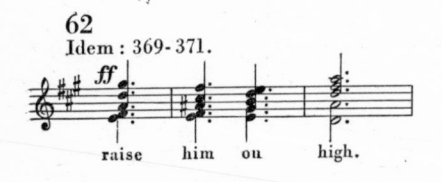

62
Idem : 369- 371.

These few bars match the 178th bar in the corresponding place in the first part, though in contrasting keys. Both represent moments of climax, but while the first is of a dissonant character and is sung by the soloist unaccompanied, the second, which is consonant, is sung by the full chorus accompanied by the orchestra. The climax is followed by a sudden drop in tempo, the colours of the orchestration begin to fade and the flame of the music dies down. Then, for the last time, the *ritornello* is heard in its original form, and as it is repeated in augmented form by the 'cellos and basses *pizzicato*, the whole tremendous work returns to silence.

160

Of the two works composed for a Latin text, the *Missa Brevis* is the more strictly liturgical in character. It is a revised version, for solo voices, mixed chorus and either organ or orchestra, of the *Mass* Kodály originally composed for solo organ—though even then its inspiration was clearly vocal. The later version was completed in 1944, during the siege of Budapest, which explains the sub-title *Tempore Belli* and gives force to the last movement, *Da Pacem*—"Give us Peace"—sung by the chorus in the name of suffering humanity. In it Kodály sums up, in his own idiom, the whole tradition of European sacred music, from Gregorian plain-song, through Palestrina and Bach, to the great romantics of the 19th century.

To the five traditional parts of the choral mass Kodály added a prefatory *Introit* and, by way of conclusion, an *Ite, Missa Est*. The former, performed by the whole orchestra, is of great majesty, and in it the theme of the *Kyrie*, one of the fundamental ideas of the whole mass, makes its appearance for the first time. The same theme, sung by the male voices and the women's voices in the lower register, accompanied by the bass strings, forms the opening to the second movement:

63

Missa Brevis: *Kyrie*, 2-4.

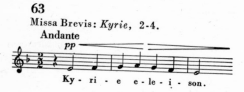

These deep, empty-sounding chords are answered by full harmonies descending from the high register:

64

Idem: 17-20.

This second theme, sung by the three soprano soloists and accompanied by the sustained notes of the high woodwind and the *tremolos* of the violins, has an almost ethereal quality; and the movement is rounded off in three-part form by the return of the *Kyrie* melody.

The *Gloria* opens with the tenor solo singing an original Gregorian melody. The principal theme is then unfolded in all its splendour by the full chorus and orchestra:

65

Missa Brevis: *Gloria*, 1-4.

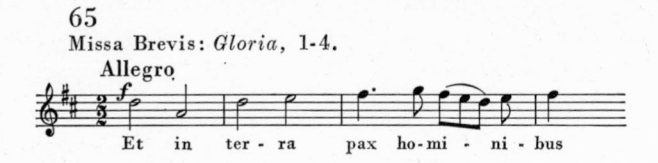

Et in ter - ra pax ho - mi - ni - bus

In the middle section, after a melody given to the soloists that expresses an extraordinary feeling of devotion (*see* below), the festive atmosphere of the first section returns:

66

Idem: 40-47.

Qui tol - lis pec - ca - ta mun - di, mi - se - re - re no - bis.

In the *Credo*, the melody has a Gregorian character, and, in the traditional way, the music here follows the meaning of the text in a literal manner: e. g. the passage where the word "consubstantial" occurs is in unison, and the words *descendit de caelis* are emphasized by a descending melodic line. The climax of this movement is reached with the harmonic tension of the *Et incarnatus est*, after which there is the resolution, carrying it forward in a jubilant song of triumph. By contrast, the devotional atmosphere of the *Sanctus* is stressed by a balance of harmonies that recalls Palestrina; and the concluding "Hosanna" is repeated in expanded form at the end of the following movement, the *Benedictus*. In the *Agnus Dei*, where the music makes the fullest use of the possibilities of the text, we hear repeated, first the melody of the *Gloria* (*see* 66th musical illustration) and then, to the words *Dona nobis pacem*, the full movement of the *Kyrie* (*see* 63rd and 64th musical illustrations). And, finally, the whole work is drawn to a close with the sublime strength of the *Ite, missa est*.

Through the return of its various sections, the *Missa Brevis* is a "compressed" bridge form of regular construction. Its axis is between the two *Hosannas* at the beginning of the *Benedictus*. The two melodies of the first unit of the bridge—the *Kyrie* and the *Qui tollis*—appear in reverse order in the *Agnus* movement of the second unit.

With the last of the three religious works, the *Te Deum of Budavár*, we come to one of the masterpieces of 20th century musical literature. Its splendid sense of proportion, the perfection of detail and the masterly way in which a balance is preserved between its various elements, make it an essentially

162

classical work; while nowhere else has Kodály so admirably succeeded in integrating into a uniquely organic unity the rich variety of styles upon which he draws.

After the opening trumpet fanfare, the chorus celebrates victory in a song of triumph:

Then, in the accompaniment to the "Te aeternum patrem" section, we hear the influence of the Hungarian instrumental style in the figures played by the high woodwind and the strings, with their racing, ascending runs; while in the "Tibi omnes angeli," which immediately follows, the series of chords, despite their essentially modern ring, recall the plagal harmonic texture of renaissance choruses:

In the triplets of the *Sanctus*, however, there is a revival of baroque word symbolism:

and this brings us to the first climax of the work, the "pleni sunt" *fugato*, in which baroque choral polyphony acquires an entirely new spirit. The pentatonic character of the theme is derived either from Gregorian chant

or from the oldest stratum of Hungarian folk music—the descending line
of the melody and the frequency of leaps of a fourth rather suggesting the
latter:

70
Idem : 43- 47.

In the concluding part of the fugato—as a symbol of pentatony—Kodály
builds up a miraculous "pillar of fourths."

With the "Te gloriosus," the high *tremolo* of the violins and the subdued
fanfares of the trumpets introduce an ethereal mood, to which the strict,
martial rhythm and ringing fortissimo of the "Te per orbem terrarum"
provides an effective contrast. Here again the emphatic leaps of a fourth
give the theme a pentatonic character; and there follows the Gregorian melody
of the "Venerandum tuum verum," which is heard, first *a cappella*, then
characteristically ornamented with *appoggiaturas* on strings and woodwind.

At this point, the whole atmosphere of the work changes: the tempo
becomes slower, the 4/4 time is replaced by 3/4, and the soloists appear for
the first time. This is the middle section, and the first part of it is built on
two contrasting themes: after the bass and tenor, the soprano solo sings a
melody, pentatonic in character and having something of the splendour of
Hungarian prosody:

71
Idem : 151 - 153.

The diatonic melody of the immediately following "Tu patris sempiternus,"
however, is the exact opposite of this, with the chorus again replacing the
soloists. These two parts, used in imitation and woven into a single unit,
lead us, with a tremendous increase in dynamics, to what is the turning-
point of the work, the section beginning with "Tu ad dexteram." Here the
tone of the words changes to one of entreaty, and as previously (*see* 71st
musical illustration) the change of mood is indicated by the use of a trio.
At this point, in order to underline the significance of the change, Kodály

164

resorts to a kind of pseudo-*reprise* by recalling the jubilant melody of the *Sanctus*. At the height of the crescendo the vigorous pentatonic theme is stated with the full weight of the whole orchestra:

72

Idem: 219-221.

Ju - dex   cre-de-ris es - se   ven - tu - rus

Then, after a breathtaking pause, the subdued entreaty of the "Te ergo quaesumus" emerges, as it were from the depths, sung first by the male choir, then taken up by the full chorus, while above its rhythmic *ostinato* we hear once again the voices of the soloists. In this section the earlier diatonic, scale-like melody is reintroduced in imitation; and the mystical theme of "Aeterna fac" and the firm pentatonic melody "Et rege eos" are respectively recollections, so to speak, of the themes of "Te gloriosus" and "Te per orbem terrarum."

This concludes the section of pseudo-*reprises*, and the authentic *reprise* begins with "Per singulos dies." To te different words, the themes of the "Te deum" and "Tibi omnes angeli" are repeated. Then new themes are introduced with the "Miserere" and "In te Domine speravi", though in the latter case the voices are still haunted by the memory of the flexible diatonic melody. It is these two themes, used in imitation, that carry us forward to the climax of the whole work, the tremendous choral *fugato*, "Non confundar." And here, with a superb sense of form, he brings back, though with changed words, the *fugato*, "Pleni sunt," which marked the climax of the first part.

These repeats, which comply not so much with the rules of musical composition as with the logic of ideas, correspond to the individual verses of the age-old hymn. Nevertheless, in essence, it is they that comprise the firm musical framework of this tremendous work, for the individual sections, though complete in themselves, constitute, when taken together in larger groupings, trio-, sonata- or rondo-form. But Kodály, with incomparable ingenuity and originality, has woven these classical forms together to create a modern "bridge-form," of which the two main supports are the twin climaxes of the "Pleni sunt" and the "Non confundar." And it is certainly no accident that both these passages, with their essentially pentatonic themes and leaps of fourths, are closely related to Hungarian folk music.

Finally, the whole tremendous drama of the *Te Deum* is brought to a close, as the incomparably lovely soprano solo breaks into the brief silence that follows the soaring ecstasy of the "Non confundar," and beneath the soft chords of the chorus the fundamental motive is heard for the last time in the dying *pizzicatos* of the bass strings. And in the beauty of these final, resounding notes it is as though we were listening to a summation of Kodály's aims: a fusion of the spirit of Hungary with that of Europe, in music that expresses his profound humanity and his confidence in the future of mankind:

73
Idem: 426-433.

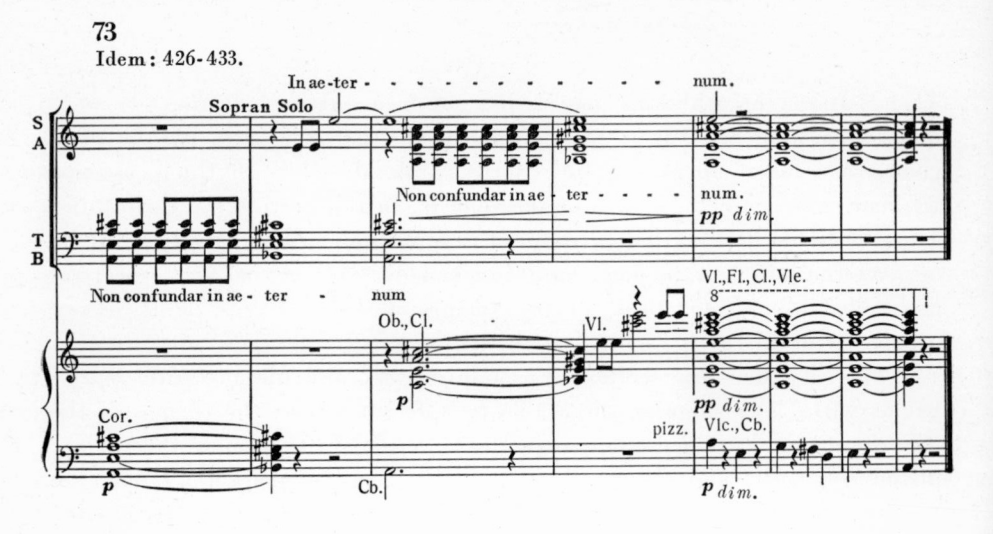

BY WAY OF EPILOGUE

Throughout this book we have endeavoured, as far as possible, to allow Kodály to speak for himself. In his case this has been all the more appropriate, since, unlike many composers, he has been a voluminous writer on a variety of subjects; and his writings tell us more about his ideas—more even about his music, perhaps—than any amount of analysis. On occasion, too, we have quoted his contemporaries, both his supporters and his opponents, for it was in the cross-fire of their opinions that his maturity as an artist was forged. Yet, as author, we ourselves have not remained completely silent. By our selection and editing of his views we have inevitably indicated our own; but, though our principal aim has been to provide some account of his manifold activities, we may hope that we have also contributed something new to the understanding of the man and the artist.

As an epigraph to the first three chapters, we might well have reprinted the following words from the book that was published as a tribute to him on his seventy-fifth birthday: "If the musical culture of Hungary has emerged from its state of semi-ignorance of fifty years ago, and is, to-day, a part of the spiritual treasury of the world, one of the noblest pledges of our status as human beings and as a nation, it is in very large measure as a result of the work of one man, Zoltán Kodály."

The final chapter, which is an independent study of his music, is an attempt to reveal the roots of his art, to trace its development, and to distinguish the main characteristics of his original and highly individual style. But here, too, we have allowed him to speak for himself, for the text is only the accompaniment, so to speak, to the musical illustrations, and it will have fulfilled its purpose if it inspires others to a more profound and penetrating study of his work.

It was not without good reason that, at the beginning of the century, Kodály evoked the hostility of conservative critics, for his music was revolutionary in its originality. To-day, a fresh debate has been provoked by the daring innovations of a younger generation of composers, which for the moment may seem to overshadow the initiative of the pioneers at the beginning of the century. But the steady glow of Kodály's noble classicism and profound humanism still persists, because its source is inexhaustible: his faith in mankind, and in the future of his own people. That faith he himself once expressed in solemn words: "It is my conviction that every nation will survive so long as it still has some message to communicate to the rest of humanity. Hungary has yet to speak her message. If she has not done so before this, it is because for centuries she has been compelled to take up arms in defence of her bare existence, for the final message of every nation can only find lasting expression in the works of peace."

NOTES

1   These words are from a poem by Endre Ady (1877-1919), a major poet, who revolution-
ized Hungarian lyric poetry.

2   In the period around 1860 Hungarian painting was strongly influenced by the school of
the Munich Academy, under Karl von Piloty (1826-1886). Many leading Hungarian
painters studied there: amongst them Mihály Munkácsy (1844-1900), Gyula Benczur
(1844-1920), and Pál Szinyei Merse (1845-1920); and mainly as a result of the work
of Benczur the Munich representational style became predominant in Budapest. The
turn of the century saw the beginnings of a new development in Hungarian painting, with
the emergence of the Nagybánya Group, led by Simon Hollósy (1857-1918), Károly
Ferenczy (1862-1917), Béla Iványi Grünwald (1867-1943), János Thorma (1870-1937)
and István Réti (1872-1945). Concerned to create a specifically Hungarian school of
painting, they succeeded, through the diversity of their individual styles, in establishing
a measure of artistic freedom; and their initiative had a stimulating effect on other
painters in Hungary.

3   Zsigmond Móricz (1879-1942), the outstanding Hungarian novelist and a pioneer of
Popular Realism.—The leading figures of the new style of poetry published their poems
in an anthology entitled *Holnap* (Tomorrow).—*Nyugat* (The West) was the name of a
literary society that was formed in 1908, with Endre Ady, Zsigmond Móricz and others,
including later also Mihály Babits (1883-1941), as its leading figures. It also was the
name of a literary journal of high artistic standing and radical outlook, which from 1908
to 1942 published the works of progressive writers.

4   Franz (Ferenc) Liszt (1811-1886) and Ferenc Erkel (1810-1893) were the two outstanding Hungarian composers of the 19th century, the latter being the first Hungarian to
write operatic music.

5   The battle of Mohács, on August 29th, 1526, was a tragic turning-point in Hungarian
history, for here, on the banks of the Danube, the Hungarian army was annihilated (and
their king, Louis II, killed) by the advancing forces of the Turkish sultan, Suleiman II.
This was the beginning of the Turkish Occupation, extending to the greater part of Hungarian territory, which was to last for more than a century and a half. Liberation was
only achieved as a result of a series of violent battles fought between 1683 and 1697;
the capital, Buda, being recaptured in 1686.

6   The Cardinal Péter Pázmány (1570-1637), one of the leaders of the Counter-Reformation
in Hungary, was a theological controversialist of great oratorical force, whose writings
did much to promote the evolution of a Hungarian prose style.

7   The modern city of Budapest is the result of the unification, in 1873, of the three towns
of Buda, Óbuda and Pest; a natural development which had been prevented for centuries
by successive wars. Under the Turkish Occupation *(see* Note 5), between 1541 and 1686,
it had been almost completely depopulated, with the result that when, after the Turks
had been driven out, the city began to grow again, its inhabitants were mostly settlers;
and, from the early 18th century onwards, the Habsburgs, in pursuance of their colonial
policy towards Hungary, ensured that these settlers were in the main Germans, Croats

and Serbs. Moreover, in the 19th century, when industrialization began to attract an influx of skilled labour to the developing city, these workers were again foreigners, since at that time the majority of Hungarians were employed in agriculture. Thus, by the time the city was becoming a modern metropolis, its population was extremely mixed and spoke a variety of languages. For many years the German population exercised a predominant influence, both in the economic and in the social life of the city, and it was not until the 20th century, that the Hungarians, growing in numbers and cultural influence, assumed the leadership. From that period onwards Budapest became the scene of a vigorous development in the national arts of Hungary.

8   Béla Reinitz (1878-1943), musician and critic, was the first composer to set some of Endre Ady's poems to music. He was Commissar for Music during the Republic of Councils (1919); and after the overthrow of the Republic went into exile in Vienna, where he became a conductor.

9   The Székelys are a Hungarian-speaking people living in the south-eastern part of Transylvania who, due to their isolated geographical situation, have preserved many ancient peculiarities in their dialect and music. Magyar, a Hungarian derivation from *Onogur*, was originally the name of one of the seven tribes, which, having been driven away from the region of the Urals by the advancing Mongols, conquered present-day Hungary in A. D. 896.

10 A literary society originally founded in memory of the author and dramatist, Károly Kisfaludy (1788-1830). From 1836 it began to undertake cultural activities neglected by the Academy of Sciences, such as publishing fiction by Hungarian writers, and papers and essays on aesthetics and the history of literature. Gradually it became more exclusive, and consequently more conservative in outlook.

11 The Csángó are a Hungarian-speaking people who live in Bucovina, Moldavia and a few, non-Székely, villages in Transylvania; i. e. regions that once formed the eastern marches of Hungary. Since 1882 several attempts have been made to settle them within the borders of present-day Hungary, and a number of them are now to be found in Western Hungary. Like the Székelys, however, the majority of them live in districts which, since the end of World War I, have belonged to Rumania.

12 Solfeggio: A method of teaching the reading and writing of music. Its Italian name is in international use. Solmization: The Hungarian version of the Curwen tonic Sol-Fa pedagogical method.

13 After World War I, the Hungarian ruling class instigated an irredentist campaign calling for the revision of the Peace Treaty. Instead of pursuing a policy of friendship with neighbouring countries, they preached a chauvinistic creed of Hungarian cultural supremacy over the Slovaks and Rumanians, whose achievements in this field they unjustly belittled. Kodály and Bartók were attacked on the grounds that the folk songs they collected were not Hungarian but Slovakian and Rumanian, for the only folk songs recognized in official circles as genuinely Hungarian were the pseudo folk songs popularized by the Gypsy orchestras. Bartók and Kodály were accused of promoting alien interests, and therefore of opposing official policy.

14 Aladár Tóth (b. 1898), a music critic and musicologist of great learning, who has been an admirer of the work of Kodály and Bartók since the nineteen-twenties. Living in exile in Stockholm during World War II, he was Director of the Budapest Opera House from 1946 to 1956. He is married to Annie Fischer, the well-known pianist.

15 Jenő Ádám (b. 1896), composer, conductor and folklorist; Professor Emeritus at the Academy of Music in Budapest.—Lajos Bárdos (b. 1899), composer and conductor; Pro-

fessor at the Academy of Music.—Géza Frid (b. 1904), Hungarian-born composer and pianist, now living in Holland.—Zoltán Horusitzky (b. 1903), composer and pianist, Professor at the Academy of Music.—György Kerényi (b. 1902), composer, conductor and musicologist; Member of the Folk-Music Research Group of the Hungarian Academy of Sciences.—Mátyás Seiber (1905-1960), Hungarian-born composer and conductor, who from the nineteen-thirties lived in Britain.—Tibor Serly (b. 1900), Hungarian-born composer, now living in the U. S. A.—Bence Szabolcsi (b. 1899), musicologist; Professor at the Academy of Music, Member of the Hungarian Academy of Sciences, and a leading authority on contemporary Hungarian music.—István Szelényi (b. 1904), composer, pianist and musicologist.—Viktor Vaszy (b. 1903), conductor and composer; Director of the Opera House at Szeged.—Zoltán Vásárhelyi (b. 1900), composer and conductor; Professor at the Academy of Music in Budapest.

16 Both the *Hymn* and the *Appeal* are age-old Hungarian national anthems: the former with words by Ferenc Kölcsey (1790-1838) and music by Ferenc Erkel (1810-1893); the latter, a poem by Mihály Vörösmarty (1800-1855), which was set to music by Béni Egressy (1814—1851). Both the words and music of the *Credo*, however, belong to the period after World War I. They are of little artistic value, and were written to support the irredentist views of the ruling class. (*See* Note 13).

17 Zsolt Harsányi (1887-1942) wrote a number of biographical novels, some of which became best sellers, particularly *The Hungarian Rhapsody*, of which the hero was Franz (Ferenc) Liszt.

18 Mihály Vörösmarty (1800-1855), a distinguished 19th century poet, and a leading figure in the political struggles of the Reform Era, which prepared the ground for the ensuing War of Independence of 1848-49.

19 *The Peacock* was originally a folk song, which expresses all the bitterness of the down-trodden peasantry. It was adapted by Endre Ady, who transformed it into a poem of revolutionary import, to which Kodály composed a forceful musical setting.

20 Until the end of World War I, Kolozsvár was the provincial capital of Transylvania, then the eastern region of Hungary, but since 1919 it has belonged to Rumania and is now known as Cluj. For a short time during World War II, however, it was returned to Hungary, under the Second Vienna Agreement between von Ribbentrop and Count Ciano, Foreign Minister of Germany and Italy respectively, as an inducement to Hungary to increase her participation in the war effort of the Axis.

21 Sándor Petőfi (1823-1849) and János Arany (*see* Note 25) were the two greatest Hungarian poets. Petőfi's revolutionary lyrics made him the poet of the War of Independence.

22 The Arrow-Cross Party was the Hungarian fascist party, so called after their emblem which was a variant of the swastika. Though it was supported by only an insignificant minority of the Hungarian people, it seized power in October 1944, with the aid of the German Army, which had occupied the country in the previous March.

23 Béla Balázs (1884-1949), poet and critic, who because of his progressive ideas and the active part he played in the Hungarian Republic of Councils in 1919, lived in exile abroad from 1919 to 1945. He wrote the libretto for Bartók's opera, *Prince Bluebeard's Castle*.

24 Albert Szenczi Molnár (1574-1634), a Calvinist theological writer, who translated the Psalms.

25 János Arany (1817-1882), the greatest Hungarian epic poet, a friend of Petőfi (*see* Note 21).

12*

26 Elemér Szentirmay (1836—1908), a composer of popular songs in imitation of genuine folk songs, some of which achieved immense popularity and have become a part of contemporary Hungarian folklore.

27 Before the First World War Hungary was a multi-national state. Its border regions were inhabited by a majority of non-Hungarian peoples: Slovaks and Ruthenians (Carpatho-Ukrainians) in the North; Rumanians in the south-east; and Croats and Serbs in the south. Living amongst these peoples, sometimes in sharply isolated groups, there was also a Hungarian population. Kodály's intention was to visit this "ethnographic border country" first, since he was convinced that the most primitive layer of folk music had survived amongst these scattered Hungarian groups. Though his opinion proved to be correct scientifically, politically it met with hostility from the ruling class, particularly after these areas, by the terms of the 1920 Peace Treaty, were annexed to Czechoslovakia, Rumania and Yugoslavia respectively; and when the Hungarian Government, intent upon recovering the lost territories, was instigating a campaign of chauvinism against the "Succession States."

28 Prince Argirus is a hero of folklore, who, after undergoing a series of miraculous adventures, finally arrives at the Fairy Castle and marries his sweetheart. The story first appears in one of the 16th century rhymed chronicles, or lays, which were mainly sung by itinerant minstrels.

29 János Horváth (1878-1961), Professor at the University of Budapest, was a leading literary scholar and authority on modern Hungarian literature.

30 Kőmíves Kelemen (Clement the Mason) is the hero of a folk tale, current in the southern and eastern parts of Hungary and in the Balkan Peninsula. Masons are building a castle, but the walls they build in the daytime collapse every night. The only way to prevent this is for one of their wives to be walled in, and Kelemen proposes that the first of the wives to arrive at the site shall be the one to be sacrificed. The tragedy is that his own wife is the first to arrive, and thus becomes the victim.

31 "Delight in tears" is a reference to the mawkish sentimentality of many of the pseudo folk songs that were written after the middle of the 19th century, and which the gypsy musicians often greatly exaggerated.

32 This was due to the fact that centuries of war and occupation had hindered the unfolding of art in Hungary. Nor had the development of art music followed a normal course, either: instead of growing out of the indigenous folk music, it took as its models the art music of other countries.

33 Hungarian prosody has its own historical peculiarities. Unlike Greek or Latin verse (though some eminent Hungarian poets have written in classical metres), or the rhymed verse and *vers libre* of Western Europe, Hungarian prosody is based primarily on stress, which is determined by the specific character of the language.

34 Pál Kadosa (b. 1903), composer and pianist; Professor at the Academy of Music in Budapest.

35 Pál Járdányi (b. 1920), composer and violinist; Member of the Folk-Music Research Group of the Academy of Sciences.

36 The choirs taking part in this movement organized inter-school choral festivals, which, because of the high quality of the music performed, were an effective means of developing musical appreciation.

37 Zoltán Gombocz (1877-1935), late Professor at the University of Budapest, was an eminent philologist who did research on the history of grammar and was editor of *The Etymological Dictionary of the Hungarian Language.*

38 *Verbunkos* Music: a Hungarian dance, with a special kind of music, which developed in connection with recruiting for the army. Its heyday was from the end of the 18th to the middle of 19th centuries. Its characteristic features are the dotted 'Hungarian' rhythm, the instrumental ornamentation and the alternation of slow and fast movements.

39 Fifth-transposition *(kvintváltó)*: a musical form, in which the second part is an exact repetition of the first, only a fifth lower, or sometimes a fifth higher.

40 Max Reger (1873-1916), a typical German composer of the late romantic school; also an organist and conductor.

41 Dániel Berzsenyi (1776-1836), the best-known poet to have written Hungarian verse in the classical Greek and Latin metres. His sublime and noble poems are filled with a deep feeling of patriotism.

42 Ferenc Kölcsey (1790-1838), poet, critic and orator. One of the outstanding personalities of the period before the 1848 War of Independence, who did much to awaken the patriotic feelings of his countrymen. Author of the Hungarian National Anthem.—Mihály Csokonai (1773-1805), lyric poet of deep feeling, who was in touch with the contemporary trends in European literature, and wrote the first Hungarian comic epic.

APPENDICES

I. KODÁLY'S PRINCIPAL MUSICAL COMPOSITIONS*

A) INSTRUMENTAL

i.) Orchestral Works

Summer Evening, 1906 (Revised 1929—30). [U. 1930]
Háry János Suite, 1927. [U.; Z.]
Theatre Overture, 1927. [U.]
Dances of Marosszék, 1930. [U. 1930; Z.]
Dances of Galánta, 1933. [U. 1934; Z.]
The Peacock, 1938—39. [sz. k. 1941; B. H.; Z.]
Concerto, 1939. [sz. k. 1942; B. H.; Z.]
Symphony, 1961. [B. H. 1962.]

ii.) Chamber Music

Adagio for Violin and Piano, 1905. [U.; R.; Z.]
Music for Piano (Op. 3), 1905-09. The Valsette, published later as a separate piece, was
    omitted from the second and later editions, which have the title Nine Pieces for Piano.
    [R. 1910; U.; Z.]
First String Quartet (Op. 2), 1908-09. [R. 1910; Z.]
Sonata for 'Cello and Piano (Op. 4), 1909-10. [U. 1921]
Duo for Violin and 'Cello (Op. 7), 1914. [U. 1922]
Sonata for 'Cello Solo, (Op. 8), 1915. [U. 1922]
Seven Piano Pieces (Op. 11), 1910-18. [U. 1921; Z.]
Second String Quartet (Op. 10), 1916-18. [U. 1921]
Serenade for Two Violins and Viola (Op. 12), 1919-20. [U. 1921]
Dances of Marosszék (For piano), 1927. [U. 1930; Z.]

iii.) Stage Works

Háry János (Op. 15), Comic Opera with libretto by Béla Paulini and the verses by Zsolt
    Harsányi (Text in Hungarian and German), 1925-27. [U. 1929 (Arrangement for piano)]
Spinning-Room, Lyrical Scenes, with folk songs from Transylvania (Text in Hungarian, Ger-
    man, English, and Italian) 1924-32. [U. 1932]

---

* In this selective bibliography the title of the work is followed by the date of composition; the date of publication
and the publisher's name, indicated by the following abbreviations, are in square brackets.

B. H. .... Boosey and Hawkes, London
M. K. .... Magyar Kórus (Hungarian Chorus), Budapest
O. U. P. .... Oxford University Press
R. .... Rózsavölgyi és Társa, Budapest
sz. k. .... published by the author
U. .... Universal A. G., Wien
Z. .... Zeneműkiadó Vállalat (Editio Musica), Budapest
Ny. K. .... Nyelvtudományi Közlemények (Review of Linguistics)

iv.) Vocal Works with Orchestral
Accompaniment

Psalmus Hungaricus (Op. 13), Text by Mihály Kecskeméti Vég, for tenor solo, mixed chorus
and orchestra (with children's chorus *ad lib.*) and organ. (Text in Hungarian, German,
English, French and Italian), 1923. [U. 1924; Z.]
Te Deum of Budavár, for solo quartet, mixed chorus, orchestra and organ, 1936. [U. 1937]
Missa Brevis, for solo voices with mixed chorus and orchestra, 1944. [B. H. 1952; Z.]
Kálló Folk Dances, for mixed chorus and folk-music orchestra (Text in Hungarian and Ger-
man), 1950. [Z. 1952; B. H.]

B) VOCAL

i.) A Cappella Choruses
Children's Choruses

The Straw Guy (Text in Hungarian, German, English and French), 1925. (sz. k. 1925; U.;
M. K.; O. U. P.; Z.]
See, the Gypsy Munching Cheese (Text in Hungarian, German, English and French), 1925.
[sz. k. 1925; U.; M. K.; O. U. P.; Z.]
St. Gregory's Day (Text in Hungarian, German, English and French), 1926. [sz. k. 1929; U.;
M. K.; O. U. P.; Z.]
Lengyel László (Text in Hungarian, German, English and French), 1927. [U. 1929; M. K.;
O. U. P.]
The Deaf Boatman, Gypsy Lament, God's Blacksmith (Text in Hungarian, German, English
and French), 1928. [sz. k.; M. K.; O. U. P.]
The Swallow's Wooing, Whitsuntide, Dancing Song, New Year's Greeting (Text in Hungarian
German, English and French), 1929. [M. K.; O. U. P.]
Epiphany (Text in Hungarian, German and English), 1933. [M. K. 1935; U.]
The Angels and the Shepherds (Text in Hungarian, German and English), 1935. [M. K. 1936;
U.; O. U. P.]

Female Voice Choruses

Two Folk Songs from Zobor (Text in Hungarian, German and English), 1908. [U. 1923]
Nights in the Mountains I—IV, (Without words), 1923-56. [In manuscript]
Four Italian Madrigals (Italian text), 1932. [sz. k. 1949; M. K.; Z.]

Male Voice Choruses

Two Male-Voice Choruses (Text in Hungarian, German and English), 1913-17. [U.; M. K.]
Songs of Karád, 1934. [M. K. 1934]
The Bachelor (Text in Hungarian and English), 1934. [M. K. 1935; B. H.]
The Ruins (Poem by Ferenc Kölcsey, in Hungarian and German), 1936. [M. K. 1936; U.]
The Peacock (Poem by Endre Ady), 1937. [M. K. 1937; B. H.; Z.]
The Son of an Enslaved Country; Still, by a Miracle, our Country Stands (Poem by Sándor
Petőfi), 1944. [M. K. 1947]

Mixed Voice Choruses

Evening (Words by Pá G   , in Hungarian, German and English), 1904. [M. K. 1931]
A Birthday Greeting (Text in Hungarian, German and English), 1931. [M. K.; U.; O. U. P.]
Mátra Pictures (Text in Hungarian, German and English), 1931. [M. K.; U.; O. U. P.; Z.]

The Aged (Words by Sándor Weöres, in Hungarian, German and English), 1933. [M. K. 1934; U.; O. U. P.; Z.]

Székely Lament, Jesus and the Traders (Text in Hungarian, German and English), 1934. [M. K. 1934; U.; O. U. P.]

Too Late (Poem by Endre Ady, in Hungarian, German and English), 1934. [M. K. 1934; U.]

Ode to Franz Liszt (Poem by Mihály Vörösmarty), Mónár Anna (Text in Hungarian, German and English), 1936. [M. K.; U.; O. U. P.]

To the Magyars (Poem by Dániel Berzsenyi), four-part canon, 1936. [M. K. 1936; Z.]

Hymn to King Stephen, 1938. [M. K.; B. H.]

Evening Song, 1938. [M. K. 1939; Z.]

Norwegian Girls (Words by Sándor Weöres), 1940. [M. K. 1940; B. H.]

The Forgotten Song of Bálint Balassi (Words by Erzsi Gazdag), 1942. [M. K.]

Cohors Generosa, 1943. [M. K.; Z.]

Dirge (Words by Pál Bodrogh), 1947. [M. K.]

Wish for Peace—The Year 1801 (Words by Benedek Virág), 1953. [Z. 1953]

Zrinyi's Appeal (For solo baritone, with Hungarian and English words), 1954. [Z. 1955]

ii.) S o n g s

Four Songs, for Voice and Piano (Text in Hungarian, German and English), 1907-17. [U. 1925; B. H.; Z.]

Songs (Op. 1), 16 Songs, for Voice and Piano (In Hungarian and English), 1907-09. [R. 1921; Z.]

Two Songs (Op. 5), for Baritone and Piano or Orchestra (In Hungarian and German), 1913-16. [U.; B. H.; Z.]

Late Melodies (Op. 6), Seven Songs for Voice and Piano (Words in Hungarian and German), 1912-16. [U. 1923; Z.]

Five Songs (Op. 9), for Voice and Piano (Words in Hungarian and German), 1915-18. [U. 1924; B. H.; Z.]

Three Songs (Op. 14), for Voice and Piano or Orchestra (Words in Hungarian, German and English), 1924-29. [U.; B. H.; Z.]

Hungarian Folk Music (57 Ballads and Folk Songs in 10 volumes), for Voice and Piano (Words in Hungarian, German and English), 1924-32. [sz. k.; R.; U.; O. U. P.; Z.]

C) EDUCATIONAL WORKS

M u s i c a l   E x e r c i s e s

15 Two-Part Exercises (Without words), 1941. [sz. k. 1941; M. K.; B. H.]

Let us Sing Correctly! Two-Part Exercises for Chorus (107 exercises without words), 1941. [sz. k. 1941; M. K.; B. H.; Z.]

Bicinia Hungarica, An Introduction to Two-Part Singing, I—IV, 1937-42. [sz. k.; M. K.; Z.]

333 Reading Exercises. An Introduction to the Folk Music of Hungary, 1943. [M. K.; Z.]

Songs for Schools, Vols. I—II, 1943. [Library of the Nation's Educators. V. 14—15]

SOL-MI, I—VIII (In collaboration with Jenő Ádám), 1944-45. [M. K.]

24 Little Canons on the Black Keys (For piano), 1945. [R. 1946; Z.]

Pentatonic Music, I—IV, 1945-48. [sz. k.; M. K.; Z.]

Song Book for Forms I—VIII in Primary Schools (8 vols., in collaboration with Jenő Ádám), 1948. [Budapest: Ministry of Religion and Public Education, 1948.]

33 Two-Part Singing Exercises; 44 Two-Part Singing Exercises; 55 Two-Part Singing Exercises, 1954. [Z. 1954]

Tricinia: 28 Three-Part Singing Exercises, 1954. [Z. 1954]
Epigrams (For voice, or instrument, and piano), 1954. [Z. 1954]

II. PRINCIPAL LITERARY WORKS

A) FOLK MUSIC RESEARCH

A magyar népdal strófaszerkezete. The Stanzaic Structure of Hungarian Folk Song. 1906 [Ny.
K. Vol. XXXVI.]
Az új egyetemes népdalgyűjtemény tervezete. A Plan for the New Universal Collection of Folk
Songs (In collaboration with Béla Bartók). 1913. [Ethnographia, Vol. XXIV. pp. 313—6.]
Ötfokú hangsor a magyar népzenében. The Pentatonic Scale in Hungarian Folk Music. 1917.
[Zenei Szemle—Musical Review Vol. I.]
Erdélyi magyarság, Népdalok. The Hungarians of Transylvania. Folk Songs (in collaboration
with Béla Bartók). 1921. [Népies Irodalmi Társaság—Society of Popular Literature—
1923.]
Nagyszalontai gyűjtés. Dallamok gyűjteménye. Dallamok jegyzetei. The Collection of Nagy-
szalonta. The Collection of Tunes. Annotation of Tunes. 1924. [Magyar Népköltési Gyűj-
temény—Hungarian Folklore Collection—Vol. XIV. Edited by Zsigmond Szendrei.]
Magyar Népzene. Hungarian Folk Music. 1931. [Zenei Lexikon—Music Lexicon—edited by
Bence Szabolcsi and Aladár Tóth.]
Néprajz és zenetörténet. Ethnography and Musical History. 1933. [Ethnographia, Vol. XLIV.]
Sajátságos dallamszerkezet a cseremisz népzenében. The Structural Peculiarities of Mari Folk
Music. 1934. [Memorial volume for the 70th birthday of József Balassa, Budapest 1934.]
A magyar népzene. The Folk Music of Hungary. 1937. [Budapest: Royal Hungarian University
Press; 2nd edition, with additions, Budapest, 1943; 3rd edition, with further additions,
and completed with a collection of examples by Lajos Vargyas, Budapest, Z. 1951; Re-
printed 1960. (German translation: Budapest, Corvina 1956; English translation: Buda-
pest, Corvina 1960.)]
Magyarság a zenében. Hungarian Musical Characteristics. 1939. *Mi a magyar?*—What is
Hungarian?—[Edited by Gyula Szekfű, Budapest; 1939.]
Népzene és műzene. Folk Music and Art Music. 1941. Squire and Peasant in Hungarian Life.
[Edited by Sándor Eckhardt, Budapest, 1941. English translation in: The 70-year-old
Zoltán Kodály, Budapest, 1952.]
Arany János népdalgyűjteménye. The Folk-Song Collection of János Arany (in collaboration
with Ágost Gyulai). 1952. [Budapest; Hungarian Academy of Sciences, 1953.]

B) MUSIC CRITICISM

Bartók's Kinderstücke. 1921. [Musikblätter des Anbruch, Wien, Vol. III.]
Béla Bartók. 1921. [La Revue Musicale, Paris, Vol. II.]
Lettera di Budapest, I—III. 1922-33. [Il Pianoforte, Torino, Vols. III—IV.]
Les Sonates de Béla Bartók. 1923. [La Revue Musicale, Paris, Vol. IV.]

C) MUSICAL EDUCATION

Gyerekkarok. Children's Choruses. 1929. [Zenei Szemle—Musical Review—Budapest, Vol. XIII.]
Zene az óvodában. Music in the Kindergarten. 1941. [Magyar Zenei Szemle—Hungarian Musical
Review—Budapest, Vol. I, No. 2.]
Magyar zenei nevelés. Hungarian Musical Education. 1945. [Ív, Pécs. Vol. I.]
Ki a jó zenész? Who is a Good Musician? 1953. [Budapest, Z. 1954.]

D) A SHORT LIST OF CRITICAL ARTICLES
AND BOOKS DEVOTED TO KODÁLY'S MUSIC

Emlékkönyv Kodály Zoltán 60. születésnapjára. In Celebration of the 60th birthday of Zoltán Kodály. [Edited by B. Gunda, Budapest, 1943.]

Emlékkönyv Kodály Zoltán 70. születésnapjára. In Celebration of the 70th birthday of Zoltán Kodály. [Zenetudományi Tanulmányok—Musical Science Studies—I, Edited by B. Szabolcsi and D. Bartha, Budapest, 1952.]

Emlékkönyv Kodály Zoltán 75. születésnapjára. In Celebration of the 75th birthday of Zoltán Kodály. [Zenetudományi Tanulmányok—Musical Science Studies—VI, Edited by B. Szabolcsi and D. Bartha, Budapest, 1957.]

M. D. Calvocoressi: *Zoltán Kodály.* [Musical Times, 1913, and Monthly Musical Record LII. 616, London, 1922.]

M. D. Calvocoressi: *Choral Music of Kodály.* [The Listener, XV. 365, London, 1936.]

M. D. Calvocoressi: *Kodály's Ballet Music.* [The Listener, XVIII. 449, London, 1937.]

A. E. F. Dickinson: *Kodály's Choral Music.* [Tempo, No. 15, London, 1946.]

L. Eősze: *Kodály Zoltán élete és munkássága.* Zoltán Kodály: His Life and Work. [Budapest, 1956.]

A. Földes: *Kodály.* [Tempo, No. 46, London, 1958.]

J. Gergely: *Zoltán Kodály, Musico Hungaro e Mestro Universal.* [Publicacoes Europa-América 1954.]

J. Gergely: *Zoltán Kodály.* [Fasquelle: Encyclopédie de la Musique II, Paris, 1959.]

E. Haraszti: *Zoltán Kodály et la musique hongroise.* [Revue Musicale, Paris, 1947.]

H. Lindlar: *Einige Kodály-Chöre.* [Musik der Zeit, 9., Bonn, 1954.]

W. H. Mellers: *Kodály and the Christian Epic.* [Studies in Contemporary Music, London, 1947.]

A. Molnár: *Kodály Zoltán.* [Népszerű Zenefüzetek—Popular Musical Booklets—4., Budapest, 1936.]

G. Pannain: *Zoltán Kodály.* [Modern Composers, London, 1932.]

M. Seiber: *Kodály: Missa Brevis.* [Tempo, No. 4, London, 1947.]

Sonkoly I.: *Kodály az ember, a művész, a nevelő* (Kodály the Man, the Artist, the Educator); [Nyíregyháza, 1948.]

B. Szabolcsi: *Die Instrumentalmusik Zoltán Kodálys.* [Musikblätter des Anbruch, Wien, 1922.]

B. Szabolcsi: *Die Lieder Zoltán Kodálys.* [Musikblätter des Anbruch, Wien, 1927, and offprint *Zoltán Kodály, ein Meister des Liedes*, U. E. Wien.]

B. Szabolcsi: *Die Chöre Zoltán Kodálys.* [Musikblätter des Anbruch, Wien, 1928.]

B. Szabolcsi: *Zoltán Kodály.* [Musik in Geschichte und Gegenwart, Bonn, 1959.]

A. Szöllősy: *Kodály művészete.* The Art of Kodály. [Budapest, 1943.]

A. Tóth: *Zoltán Kodály.* [Revue Musicale, X, 9, Paris, 1929.]

D. Tóth: *Un musicista ungherese: Zoltán Kodály.* [Corvina, Budapest, 1938.]

L. Vargyas: *Zoltán Kodály.* [Ungarn, II. 12, Budapest, 1942.]

J. S. Weissmann: *Kodály, Zoltán.* [Grove's Dictionary of Music and Musicians, Fifth Ed., Edited by Eric Blom, Vol. IV, 795—805, London, 1954.]

J. S. Weissmann: *Kodály's Later Orchestral Music.* [Tempo No. 17, London, 1950. The same in German: Musik der Zeit, 9, Bonn, 1954.]

F. Wildgans: *Zoltán Kodály, ein ungarischer Volksmusiker.* [Rondo, Österreichische Musikzeitschrift, No. 1, Wien 1953.]

INDEX